IN THE FIELD WITH

NATIONAL GEOGRAPHIC

IN THE FIELD WITH

NATIONAL GEOGRAPHIC

THE INSIDE STORY OF LEGENDARY EXPLORERS, EDUCATORS, SCIENTISTS, AND STORYTELLERS

NATIONAL GEOGRAPHIC

◂ 1997 Suspended above Antarctica's breathtaking Queen Maud Land, Conrad Anker uses a mechanical ascender to scale a previously unclimbed peak nicknamed the Razor. The landscape looked "so alien we felt as if we should be wearing space suits," said Jon Krakauer of the expedition.

This book includes images and descriptions of hominin remains. Hominin remains include both direct and close human relatives.

ographic Society U.S.A.
PHOTO - SURVEY

CONTENTS

◂ 1947 Told to "do India," photographer Volkmar Wentzel spent nearly two years traveling the subcontinent and logged more than 40,000 miles in his rehabbed WWII ambulance. The truck served as a mobile hotel, darkroom, and billboard advertising his adventure.

INTRODUCTION

MISSION FORWARD

As a social scientist, I've long relied on data to make a point. But one of the most meaningful lessons I've learned as CEO of the National Geographic Society is this: When it comes to bringing critical issues to the forefront—to commanding attention and inspiring action—what's most impactful isn't data. It's awe.

I learned this lesson when National Geographic Explorer Sylvia Earle shared with me the story of her solo descent in the Pacific Ocean. In 1979, with years of scientific training behind her, Sylvia asked: Could a suit like those worn in space help us study the deep sea? The hulking JIM suit in question was built for underwater construction and salvage, not research. But that's what made the experiment so emblematic: Exploration demands stepping into the unfamiliar. And so, Sylvia did.

She walked the seafloor 1,250 feet below the surface—deeper than any human in history. With scientific precision and poetic prose, Sylvia wrote in the May 1980 issue of *National Geographic* magazine: "Tiny luminescent creatures eddy and swirl like living constellations. I feel a sense of freedom in the eternal night that mantles the ocean realm."

▼ **1979** After descending on the nose of a submarine, Sylvia Earle walks untethered on the seafloor, 1,250 feet deep, setting a record that still stands today.

That moment was magnetic: The otherworldliness, the quiet courage, the pursuit of science steeped not in fanfare, but in wonder. That's one thing I love about National Geographic. We don't just document a moment. We open a door and invite the world in.

Since 1888, the Society has championed thousands of audacious Explorers and evolved to amplify their unique messages to more people, more powerfully. We began with public lectures. Then published a magazine. We shared stories through films, TV specials, and global channels. We streamed into classrooms and onto smartphones, building one of the largest social media communities on Earth. Today, our stories reach millions more through Disney+.

The next bold expression of our mission is the National Geographic Museum of Exploration, a living, breathing space where you don't just learn about Explorers, you also feel what they feel: curiosity, possibility, resolve. Inside is a replica of Sylvia's iconic suit, painstakingly re-created to honor her feat—a record she still holds. Isn't that extraordinary? Her sense of wonder and determination to share it continue to captivate me.

I remain convinced of the crucial role of research and data in shaping the world. But I've come to believe it's awe that inspires us to change it. Awe stirs something deeper: a pull to dream beyond boundaries. Whenever I've followed that feeling, it's led me somewhere worthwhile.

Where will it lead you?

—Jill Tiefenthaler
CEO, National Geographic Society

PROLOGUE

AN INVITATION TO EXPLORE

"The members of our Society will not be confined to professional geographers, but will include that large number who, like myself, desire to promote special researches by others, and to diffuse the knowledge ... so that we may all know more of the world upon which we live."

GARDINER GREENE HUBBARD

◂ 1905 Photographs of isolated Lhasa, Tibet—including this Buddhist temple—appeared in the January 1905 issue of *National Geographic,* delighting readers and launching a tradition of photo-first articles.

▲ **1888** The 33 founders of the National Geographic Society first met at the Cosmos Club in Washington, D.C., on January 13, 1888. This 1963 painting depicts the group as older than they were at the time of the talks (possibly to convey a sense of solemnity, or the artist may have lacked photographs of his subjects from that time). They are shown in discussions to establish an organization dedicated to "the increase and diffusion of geographical knowledge." The round table is still used in the Society's headquarters today.

From the top of Mount Everest to the depths of the sea, from the world beneath the microscope to the stars in distant galaxies, National Geographic has long used the "power of science, exploration, education, and storytelling to illuminate and protect the wonder of our world." Informed by a community of explorers from around the globe and a tradition of pushing the boundaries of storytelling, the organization continues to inspire its ever growing audience to spark their sense of wonder.

The seed for this audience was planted in Washington, D.C., on January 13, 1888. A group of 33 of the city's scientific and intellectual leaders met at the Cosmos Club on that chilly night to consider "the advisability of organizing a society for the increase and diffusion of geographical knowledge."

They were an energetic lot, with widely ranging professions as geologists, geographers, meteorologists, cartographers, bankers, lawyers, naturalists, soldiers, and sailors. What they had in common was the desire to promote scientific study and make the results available to the public. Many were in their 20s and 30s and were actively pursuing careers that took them to places far removed from the smoky, high-ceilinged Cosmos Club. They wandered far and wide in the pursuit of science. But each autumn they returned to Washington from fieldwork posts in the deserts of the West, the forests of Alaska, or far out on the oceans.

▲ **1888** Gardiner Greene Hubbard, the Society's first President, signed the original invitation to the Cosmos Club (below).

At the time, Washington, D.C., was home to most of the federal government's leading scientific bureaus: the U.S. Geological Survey, the Coast and Geodetic Survey, the Navy Hydrographic Office, and the Smithsonian Institution, to name a few. These institutions became partners as data was analyzed, results were written up, and funding was sought for another season in the field, helping to transform wintertime Washington into a vibrant city of intellectual activity.

These founders embodied the spirit of adventure and discovery that has come to be associated with the National Geographic Society. Among their ranks were John Wesley Powell, known for his exploration of the Grand Canyon, and Adolphus W. Greely, chief signal officer of the U.S. Army and a noted polar explorer who in 1881 had led an expedition to Canada's Lady Franklin Bay. Though one of his men achieved a new "farthest north" mark, Greely's expedition ended tragically—just five of 25 men survived being marooned for three years without resupply, and Greely himself was rescued within

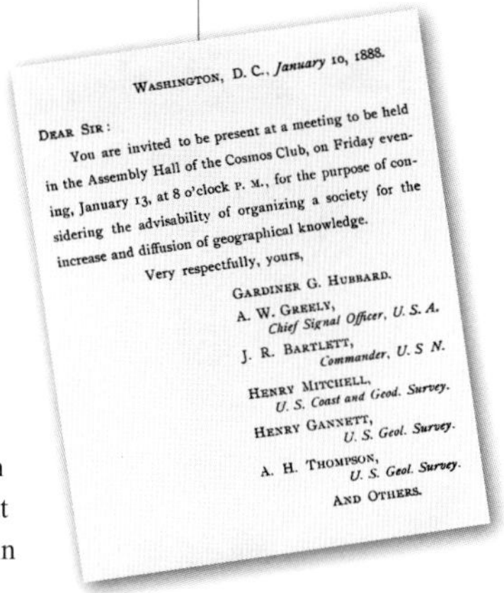

WASHINGTON, D. C., *January* 10, 1888.

DEAR SIR:

You are invited to be present at a meeting to be held in the Assembly Hall of the Cosmos Club, on Friday evening, January 13, at 8 o'clock P. M., for the purpose of considering the advisability of organizing a society for the increase and diffusion of geographical knowledge.

Very respectfully, yours,

GARDINER G. HUBBARD.
A. W. GREELY, *Chief Signal Officer, U. S. A.*
J. R. BARTLETT, *Commander, U. S. N.*
HENRY MITCHELL, *U. S. Coast and Geod. Survey.*
HENRY GANNETT, *U. S. Geol. Survey.*
A. H. THOMPSON, *U. S. Geol. Survey.*
AND OTHERS.

▲ **1877** Founder Clarence Dutton surveyed the Grand Canyon region. Adolphus Greely (below) explored the Arctic.

hours of certain death. Grove Karl Gilbert, the nation's leading geologist, was also at the Cosmos Club meeting, as was Henry Gannett, a distinguished cartographer. George Kennan, a former telegraph operator, had spent years living in Siberia and wrote a book about the experience. Kennan was the lone representative of a profession, journalism, that likely most of the others thought would be of little relevance in the new organization's future.

Two weeks after the first meeting at the Cosmos Club, the founders elected lawyer and financier Gardiner Greene Hubbard the first President of the fledgling National Geographic Society. Though not a scientist himself, Hubbard had a keen interest in science and was a staunch supporter of scientific research; most notably, he financed and promoted the experiments of his son-in-law, Alexander Graham Bell, who had invented the telephone in 1875.

In his introductory speech, Hubbard emphasized his lack of scientific training, declaring, "By my election, you notify the public that the members of our Society will not be confined to professional geographers, but will include that large number who, like myself, desire to promote special researches by others, and to diffuse the knowledge so gained, among men, so that we may all know more of the world upon which we live."

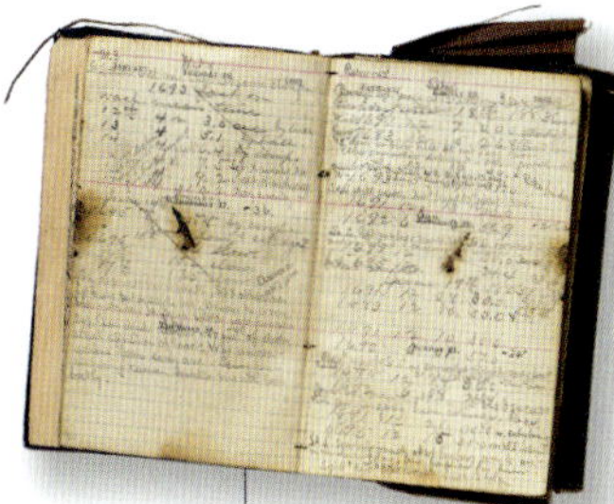

▲ **1881** Adolphus Greely's battered diary bears witness to his Arctic hardships.

▼ **1885** George Kennan's writings on Russia exposed the cruelties of the tsar's regime.

As the new National Geographic Society set these lofty goals, the United States was about to enter a great era of innovation and discovery. In 1888 Thomas Edison invented the kinetoscope, a prototype for motion pictures, and George Eastman perfected the box camera and black-and-white roll film. Automobiles and airplanes would soon become new means of transportation, and telegraphs and telephones were beginning to change the way people communicated.

Though much of the world remained to be explored, scientists were amassing knowledge on a tremendous scale. An enormous amount of energy and optimism was afoot, as was the passionate belief that science had the power to correct many of the social and economic defects of a society entering the modern era.

The National Geographic Society would be a force in this scientific evangelism, and many scientific associations of the period shared its vision. But what would set the organization apart was its ageless appeal to the explorer in all of us. That has allowed it to become what it is today: a global nonprofit providing a window on the wonders of the world and influencing the lives of millions. ■

CHAPTER 1

1888 - 1920

THE WORLD AND ALL THAT IS IN IT

"The world and all that is in it is our theme, and if we can't find anything to interest ordinary people in that ... we better shut up shop."

ALEXANDER GRAHAM BELL

◂ 1909 Portrait of explorer Robert E. Peary

CIRCA 1900 Whenever the cherry trees flowered in Japan, Eliza Scidmore set up her camera, for the trembling blossoms "filled the people with joy."

▲ **1891** Civil War veteran, geologist, explorer, and Society founder John Wesley Powell pauses on horseback near Flagstaff, Arizona. At age 35 Powell led the first expedition by boat down the Colorado River through the Grand Canyon.

The first issue of *National Geographic,* published in October 1888, was a modest-looking scientific brochure with an austere terra-cotta cover. The featured article was a dense, scholarly report by W.J. McGee, "The Classification of Geographic Forms by Genesis." Yet also tucked into the issue was an account of the Great Blizzard of March 11–14, which opened with isotherms and meteorological charts but ended in a riveting description of the survival of the New York–based pilot boat *Charles H. Marshall.* From the start the magazine presented an interesting mix of science and adventure.

While it had neither a paid staff nor an official headquarters, the Society was determined to influ-

◂ **1888** The first issue of *National Geographic* magazine appeared in October 1888 and was sent to the Society's nearly 200 members. It contained mostly reprints of papers that had been presented at recent meetings.

ence the world of geography. It successfully lobbied to establish the U.S. Board on Geographic Names, which in 1890 began untangling the confusion of place-names scattered over the map of the continent. The Society also began presenting gold medals for outstanding student essays on geography. And at the 1893 Chicago World's Fair, National Geographic sponsored the first international meeting of geographers ever held in America.

▲ **1891** Society lectures quickly became popular Washington events. Above, a ticket from Robert Peary's lecture on his Greenland expedition. Proceeds from his lectures helped Peary fund his expeditions to the Arctic.

In the era before television and movies, when travel was still a luxury reserved for the well-to-do, the National Geographic Society delivered a world of adventure to its Washington, D.C., members by inviting prominent explorers and scientists to the capital to speak about their work. In February 1888, just one month after the Society's founding, explorer John Wesley Powell inaugurated the lecture series by delivering a talk about the physical geography of the United States.

▲ **1913** Polar explorers and other Society luminaries gathered at the Society to present Roald Amundsen with a medal for being the first to reach the South Pole.

Very quickly the Society began attracting scientists and adventurers eager to tell their stories, including Fridtjof Nansen, an Arctic explorer; Gifford Pinchot, founder of the U.S. Forest Service; and mountaineer Annie S. Peck, who told of climbing peaks in the Alps and volcanoes in Mexico. Thousands gathered to hear Roald Amundsen, soon to be the first man to reach the South Pole, discuss his pioneering navigation of the Northwest Passage.

In 1889 *National Geographic* published its first color illustrations—pastel drawings of scenes from Nicaragua—as well as the first authoritative four-color foldout map, which would soon

▲ **1890** Gripping their alpenstocks, members of the Society's first expedition begin exploring Alaska's Mount St. Elias. William Lindsley's journal (below) records their harrowing attempts to summit the mountain.

become an important part of the magazine. And in the spring of 1890 the two-year-old Society sponsored its first expedition into the field, teaming up with the U.S. Geological Survey.

Ten men, led by geologist Israel C. Russell, explored and surveyed Mount St. Elias, the highest point on the boundary between Alaska and Canada. The expedition set the pattern for the Society's expeditions to come, as well as the tone of the magazine's first-person adventure-narrative accounts. "Darkness settled and rain fell in torrents," Russell wrote, "beating through our little tent. We rolled ourselves in blankets, determined to rest in spite of the storm. Avalanches, already numerous, became more frequent. A crash told of tons of ice and rock sliding down on the glacier."

Membership in these early years was largely men in scientific circles of Washington and their families and friends and included a growing number of women but was restricted based on race. A volunteer committee edited the magazine, which faithfully listed the names of the Society's several hundred members in each issue, reported the minutes of their meetings, and even documented group picnics and field trips to nearby Civil War battlefields. It also ran a number of articles that, as one journalist later observed, "were suitable for diffusing geographic knowledge among those who already had it and scaring off the rest."

▾ **1912** Proud to support science and exploration, people often displayed membership certificates in their homes.

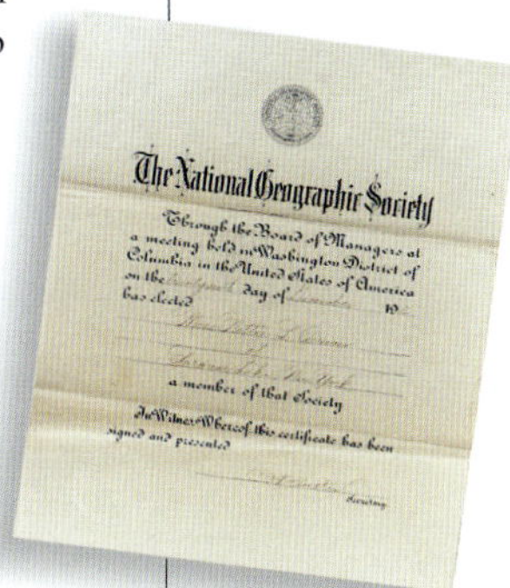

The magazine, published only sporadically, floundered commercially. In 1896 the Board of Managers—hoping to boost circulation—placed the *Geographic* on newsstands, began to solicit advertising, and made the 25-cent journal into an "illustrated monthly" in imitation of the day's more successful magazines, *Harper's Weekly* and *Munsey's.* John Hyde, a statistician with the Department of Agriculture, became Editor and began to insert an occasional photograph, a practice some prominent members considered frivolous.

Despite such grumblings, in 1896 Hyde published a photograph unlike any other then printed by an American magazine. It was a wedding photo: A Zulu bride and groom hold hands, and they're both topless. This bold move—to show people as they lived, even if it differed from American expectations—would become characteristic of the magazine.

▾ **1890** Although a photograph of a map had appeared in an earlier issue, this modest image of Russia's Herald Island published in July 1890 was the first photograph of a natural scene in the magazine.

In 1897 Gardiner Greene Hubbard died and his son-in-law Alexander Graham Bell was elected to the office of President. Inventor of the telephone, pioneer of flight, proponent of oralism in deaf education, he was nearly 51 years old and fully immersed in a number of scientific projects. He was reluctant to take the job. But the organization was on the brink of bankruptcy. Bell agreed to lead the Society, as he later wrote in his journal, only "in order to save it."

▲ **1900** Society President Alexander Graham Bell prepares to view a total eclipse of the sun during a National Geographic excursion to Norfolk, Virginia, on May 28, 1900. Most of the Society's few hundred members participated in the trip.

Bell had a number of ideas. He told the governing board he wanted to cultivate *members* of a Society, rather than readers of a magazine. Do not depend on fickle newsstand sales; subscriptions to *National Geographic* should come only with membership, he said. Shrewdly, Bell emphasized the founders' wishes: Not just the scientific elite, but schoolteachers, nurses, construction workers, and salesmen might be interested in funding expeditions to Peru and dispatching explorers to the South Pole.

Bell also insisted that these new members should actually be able to read and enjoy the articles. He wanted no more obtuse and undecipherable academic tracts. And, what's more, he insisted on "pictures, and plenty of them."

To help implement his new ideas, Bell cast about for a full-time editor who could relieve the overtaxed John Hyde. He soon encountered Gilbert Hovey Grosvenor, 23 years old, an instructor at a boys' academy in New Jersey. His father, noted historian Edwin A. Grosvenor, had lectured at the Society a few years earlier and had visited the Bells.

▸ **1899** Recent Amherst graduate Gilbert H. Grosvenor, pictured at his desk decades later, began working at the National Geographic Society on April 1, 1899. He would remain at his post for another 55 years.

When Gilbert Grosvenor arrived in Washington for an interview, Bell pushed copies of the nation's best magazines—*McClure's, Munsey's, Harper's Weekly*—in front of him and asked, "Can you create a geographic magazine as popular as these, one that will support the Society instead of the Society being burdened with the magazine?"

Grosvenor answered yes.

Bell hired Grosvenor as the magazine's assistant editor, at the salary of $100 a month paid out of Bell's pocket, and on April 1, 1899, took him to the rented quarters where the Geographic shared an office with the American Forestry Society. Grosvenor found that the entire inventory of the National Geographic Society comprised "two rickety chairs, a small table, a litter of papers and ledgers, and six enormous boxes crammed with *Geographics* returned by the newsstands."

Gilbert Grosvenor was the Society's first full-time employee, and the job he had just undertaken would consume his energy for a lifetime. To boost membership, he sent letters to prominent Washington men to "nominate their friends" for *election* to membership, making sure the letters were on expensive, embossed paper. The flattery recruited many, and membership took an upturn.

▲ **1900s** A strong and often vocal supporter of women's right to vote, Elsie May Bell Grosvenor (she married Gilbert Grosvenor) was involved in many Society activities and designed the first Society flag in 1903. Its bands of green, brown, and blue (below) represent sea, Earth, and sky.

Under Grosvenor *National Geographic* magazine covered a world of topics ranging from Korea to British shipbuilding to Robert E. Peary's latest Arctic expedition to measuring the height of Mount Rainier. He took as his editorial cue a directive he once received from Bell: "the world and all that is in it is our theme, and if we can't find anything to interest ordinary people in that subject we better shut up shop and become a strict, technical, scientific journal for high class geographers and geological experts."

Bell preferred popular, readable coverage on geographic topics. When news of the 1902 eruption of Mount Pelée on Martinique reached Washington, Grosvenor telegraphed Bell, who was vacationing in Nova Scotia, and sought

ELIZA SCIDMORE

Eliza Scidmore (1856–1928) shattered barriers as the National Geographic Society's first woman officer, editor, and board member. She was a passionate traveler fascinated by Asian cultures. Scidmore wrote 17 captivating articles and contributed color photographs (including the hand-tinted depiction of a Japanese rice farmer below) to the magazine. Her work transported readers to distant lands.

approval to send a small scientific team to the island to investigate the eruption. Bell declined, telling the young Editor, "Go yourself to Martinique in the interests of the Magazine and I will pay your expenses ... this is the opportunity of a lifetime—seize it. Start within 24 hours and let the world hear from you as our representative. Leave science to others and give us details of living interest beautifully illustrated by photographs."

Although Grosvenor did not go—a Society-sponsored expedition did—the point was made: *National Geographic* magazine should combine vivid storytelling with striking photographs.

Grosvenor constantly monitored public opinion and looked for ways to boost interest in the magazine. He used the Society's popular lecture series as a barometer to gauge interest in subjects and illustrations. Arcane addresses on topography or land use drew an average of 20 attendees. But on the night that a scientist who had gone to Martinique lectured on the eruption of Mount Pelée, the 1,200-seat theater was packed. Unfortunately, the speaker brought no illustrations. Grosvenor overheard two young women complain: "Why doesn't he show photographs? That's what we want."

Grosvenor needed no further convincing. After all, photography was a frank, scientific way of looking at the world, although many intellectuals continued to dismiss it as superficial, if not vulgar. Undeterred, Grosvenor began energetically scouring the city for photo collections and archives. In 1903 the

▲ **1900s** Father-in-law Bell and two of Grosvenor's children pay a visit to the Editor at Beinn Bhreagh, the family's summer home in Baddeck, Nova Scotia. Grosvenor often retreated from the hubbub to the solitude of this tent, where he edited articles for *National Geographic,* sending the finished manuscripts back to Washington.

Society moved to its first headquarters building, Hubbard Hall, six blocks north of the White House on 16th Street. Grosvenor became both full-fledged Editor and Director of Society Operations. Soon after, Alexander Graham Bell stepped down as President. Though retired, he never lost interest in the magazine, sending his son-in-law packages of story ideas and photographs while contributing articles, often on tetrahedral kites or other strange flying machines. Bell continued offering pertinent editorial advice, once noting, "The features of most importance are the illustrations … The disappointing feature of the Magazine is that there is so little in the text about the pictures … It seems to me that one notable line for improvement would be either to adapt the pictures to the text or the text to the pictures. Why not the latter?"

The NATIONAL GEOGRAPHIC MAGAZINE

PRESENT CONDITIONS IN CHINA

THE GREATEST HUNT IN THE WORLD

LATIN AMERICA AND COLOMBIA

▸ **1906** The art nouveau design on the cover of the December *Geographic* was the fifth cover format since 1888. In 1910 the magazine assumed its familiar oak-and-laurel-leaved look, the basis for the yellow border of today.

It was prescient advice. In late 1904, when the printer told him he had to quickly fill 11 pages, Grosvenor reached for a package that had just arrived from Buriat Tsybikoff and Kalmuck Norzunoff of the Imperial Russian Geographical Society. Inside were rare photographs of Lhasa, Tibet, among the least accessible cities in the world. Picking out a dozen, he sent them to the printer with only brief photo captions, adapting the text to the pictures. Knowing this was close to heresy for a serious magazine, he feared he might be fired. But when the January 1905 issue appeared, friends, even strangers, stopped him on the street offering congratulations.

▲ **1895** Portrait of explorer Robert E. Peary as a young man

▼ **1909** Guides, sled dogs, and crew crowd the deck of Peary's ship on "a mild day."

Three months later, in the April 1905 *Geographic,* Grosvenor published a staggering 138 photographs of the Philippines obtained free from the U.S. government through his

cousin, William Howard Taft, former U.S. commissioner for the Philippines and soon to be president of the United States. The issue was so popular it was soon reprinted.

In July 1906 Grosvenor devoted an entire issue to wildlife: "Photographing Wild Game with Flashlight and Camera," written and shot by George Shiras 3d, a former U.S. congressman who had replaced his hunting gun with a camera. Seventy-four candid photographs captured animals—deer, porcupines, and a lynx—as they tripped across triggers in the darkness. Shiras's photos caused a sensation. President Theodore Roosevelt was enthralled, and letters poured in from readers demanding more natural history. The impact of photos was now beyond dispute. In two years, membership had jumped from 3,000 to 20,000. The National Geographic Society had become the largest geographic organization on the globe.

Grosvenor never looked back. Using photography as his lens on the world, he filled the pages of the magazine with wonders: Egyptian tombs, Chinese canals, Canadian Rockies, even backyard insects. At times, the magazine's coverage reflected an American perspective and did not align with the communities' own perspectives and stories. The July 1907 issue featured some of the photographic portraits of Native Americans made by Edward Curtis, who spent a lifetime documenting the tribes of the American West.

▲ **1909** Peary often carried a lightweight, portable roll-film camera on his Arctic expeditions.

32 The National Geographic Magazine
Views of Lhasa 33

▼ **1905** The January 1905 *Geographic* held a surprise—11 full pages of photos, the magazine's first picture story. The issue's popularity confirmed Grosvenor's faith in the editorial value of photography.

THE ENDS OF THE EARTH

EXPLORING THE POLES

▲ **1921** Men and dogs cross treacherous ice floes in the Arctic on the MacMillan Expedition.

▼ **1926** The sun compass designed for Richard Byrd's polar flights

"That imaginary point—the aloof and lonely bottom of the earth" was how Richard E. Byrd described the South Pole. In 1888, when the National Geographic Society was founded, both poles did seem more imaginary than real, mere blanks on the world map. But the Society came of age during one of the great eras in polar exploration.

The commanding figure of Robert E. Peary was the Geographic's original polar hero. The Society championed his claim to have been first to reach the North Pole on April 6, 1909, and showered Peary with grants and gold medals during his lifetime—but not the men who accompanied him: Matthew Henson, Ootah, Seegloo, Egingwah, and Ooqueah. Henson was finally awarded the Hubbard

Medal in 2000, 45 years after his death.

National Geographic also warmly welcomed to its headquarters Sir Ernest Shackleton, the legendary Antarctic explorer, and Roald Amundsen, the first to reach the South Pole. In 1925 Donald MacMillan led a Society expedition that was the first to use airplanes and shortwave radio to explore the Arctic.

◂ **1957** On assignment to Antarctica, staff photographer Thomas J. Abercrombie—the first journalist to reach the South Pole—scrapes ice from his beard at the International Geophysical Year's South Pole station. That evening, the temperature dropped to minus 102.1°F.

In Richard E. Byrd the Geographic found a second polar hero. In 1926 Byrd and a copilot may have been first to fly over the North Pole, a feat made possible by a navigational sun compass provided him by the Society. Three years later, in 1929, carrying both the sun compass and a National Geographic flag, Byrd and four companions became the first to fly over the South Pole as well.

The heroic age of polar exploration has given way to one of aircraft, icebreakers, and permanent research stations. Yet determined individuals with dogsleds still occasionally slog over the ice and into the pages of *National Geographic*. One is Will Steger, first to lead dogsled teams both to the North Pole and across the vast extent of Antarctica. In 1995 Steger became the Society's first Explorer in Residence. ■

▾ **1909** The diagonal patch missing from Peary's flag was ripped off and left at the North Pole.

▲ **1911** A group of Piegan Native Americans makes camp in a blooming prairie beside a lake.

Paintings occasionally supplemented photographs. "Fifty Common Birds of Farm and Orchard," published in June 1913, was originally printed as an agricultural pamphlet. Grosvenor, fast becoming a passionate bird-watcher, borrowed the color plates with their exquisite paintings of birds. The result was an issue so popular that for many years birds were a perennial staple in the magazine.

The success of *National Geographic* meant increased support for exploration and discovery. In 1907 the Society awarded a grant to Cmdr. Robert E. Peary in support of his forthcoming attempt to reach the North Pole. Peary had already made several arduous treks north; for these pioneering explorations the Society presented him with the first Hubbard Medal, its highest honor. Standing on feet severely impacted by frostbite at the Society's annual white-tie banquet, the determined Peary accepted the medal from President Theodore Roosevelt and vowed to reach his goal. For the true explorer, Peary said, "The thing he has set himself to do is a part of his very being."

▲ CIRCA **1900** Photographing themselves, white-tailed deer trip a wire connected to a camera. These are the first nighttime nature shots ever published in the magazine. George Shiras 3d, naturalist and photographer, was internationally recognized for his work.

Two years later, on April 6, 1909, Peary and his crew, including the skilled African American explorer Matthew Henson and Inuit team members Ootah, Seegloo, Egingwah, and Ooqueah, arrived at the top of the world. Or at least Peary claimed that they did. Frederick A. Cook's rival boast—that he had reached the pole a year earlier—was dismissed for lack of evidence. Though a Society committee concluded that

◀ **1911** This sprawling, eight-foot foldout panorama of the Canadian Rockies, the longest supplement ever published in the magazine, appeared in the June 1911 *Geographic*.

▲ **1909** Robert E. Peary's North Pole team: Ooqueah, Ootah, Matthew Henson, Egingwah, and Seegloo

▼ **1912** Two years before the Panama Canal opened to traffic, the magazine published this bird's-eye view map.

Peary did get there, and nearly every geographic body in the world subsequently agreed, doubts still linger.

By 1912 the Society had grown strong enough to record a $43,000 surplus, which was earmarked specifically for the support of scientific exploration. Soon the Geographic became one of the nation's primary sponsors of scientific expeditions, and the magazine became the publication of record for discovery. Furthermore, the Society continued to honor prominent explorers and scientists. In 1910 it bestowed its Hubbard Medal on Sir Ernest Shackleton for coming within 112 miles of the South Pole, and in 1913 it conferred a special gold medal on Roald Amundsen for being first to actually arrive there.

▲ **1910** Battling the ice pack at Alaska's Disenchantment Bay, glaciologists Ralph S. Tarr and Lawrence Martin led this expedition to map and monitor fluctuations in numerous glaciers. Their research, based on three separate expeditions, was published by the Society in 1914 as a book that guided glacier research for decades and helped scientists understand North America's ice ages.

One of the most exciting Society-sponsored expeditions was Hiram Bingham's search among the highlands of Peru for a legendary Inca capital. After local guides led Bingham to the astonishing abandoned Inca city of Machu Picchu, the dramatic story of his quest and excavations filled all 186 pages of the April 1913 issue. In 1915 Robert Griggs explored Alaska's Mount Katmai Peninsula, the scene three years earlier of the largest volcanic eruption of the 20th century. The Society eventually awarded grants for six expeditions to the area, part of which was fissured with spectacular steam vents. Griggs named that region the Valley of Ten Thousand Smokes, and it was later designated a national monument.

When in 1916 the Society interceded with money to help preserve an important stand of California sequoias, it had already been urging the conservation of natural resources for years. For decades to come the Society would work closely with the National Park Service, which the Society helped establish in 1916, and other agencies dedicated to preserving wilderness.

World War I underscored the growing national reach and importance of the *Geographic*. Readers opened their August 1914 edition of the magazine to

▸ **1913** "Fifty Common Birds of Farm and Orchard" in the June 1913 *Geographic* contained 50 full-color bird portraits by Louis Agassiz Fuertes, the magazine's first showcase of the famous illustrator's work.

EXPEDITIONS

THE HEART OF NATIONAL GEOGRAPHIC

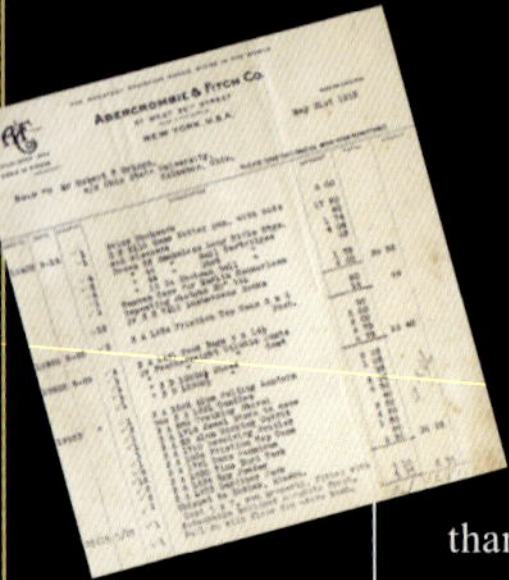
ABERCROMBIE & FITCH CO.
NEW YORK, U.S.A.

▲ **1912** The supply list for the Griggs expedition includes powdered eggs and Lumberman socks.

In 1890 Israel C. Russell led the Society's first expedition to map Mount St. Elias in Alaska. Since then the National Geographic Society has funded more than 15,000 grants for research and expeditions to almost every corner of the globe. Formalized as the Committee for Research and Exploration in 1916, the CRE gathers a board of distinguished scientists to review applications and grant funds to scientists from all over the world. After conducting fieldwork, grantees write up their findings and send reports to Society headquarters. Some of their results may be featured in *National Geographic* magazine or in National Geographic's books, on the website, or on television.

▲ **2024** Trained as a biologist, photographer Thomas P. Peschak spent more than a year documenting the world's most diverse rainforest—the Amazon—and the scientists studying it.

Through Society sponsorship, William Beebe and Otis Barton made their pioneering half-mile ocean descent in a steel bathysphere (1934) and Jane Goodall ventured into the African forest to study chimp behavior (1961). The CRE supported Robert Ballard's Black Sea work, which uncovered well-preserved Greek and Roman ships and traces of an ancient, cataclysmic flood. Grants have supported Nizar Ibrahim's excavation of a nearly complete *Spinosaurus* as well as the Photo Ark, photographer Joel Sartore's project to document every species living in zoos, aquariums, and wildlife sanctuaries. ■

◂ **1918** Using *National Geographic* magazine as a classroom text, a military instructor teaches English to foreign-born soldiers at Camp Kearny, California.

find an up-to-date map of "The New Balkan States and Central Europe" that allowed them to follow the developments of the war. Large maps of the fighting fronts continued to be published throughout the conflict, and *National Geographic* kept members informed of the history and culture of the warring countries with articles on "The World's Debt to France," "Belgium's Plight," and "The German Nation." It featured stories on conditions at the front, including the prevalence of "cooties" (lice), as well as a special issue, praised by President Woodrow Wilson, on the flags and iconography of the world. The Society established a News Service Bureau to provide bulletins on the geographic aspects of the war for the nation's newspapers. Furthermore, it supported a hospital ward near Paris for wounded soldiers and allowed Red Cross workers to roll bandages in the Society's library.

In 1920 the Board of Trustees elected Gilbert Hovey Grosvenor as both President and Editor. After two decades of struggle, the Society was financially stable, with a permanent staff and headquarters. As the nation slipped into the jazzed-up roaring '20s, Alexander Graham Bell died in 1922 at the age of 75. By then the formerly austere little scientific journal had become one of America's most trusted and eagerly anticipated magazines. ■

▾ **1917** "Flags of the World" issue, October 1917

CHAPTER 2

1921-1956

BRINGING COLOR TO THE WORLD

"It was only after my return from a first visit to Japan after seeing the old cherry trees, in their glory, that any idea moved me."

ELIZA SCIDMORE

◂ CIRCA 1925 **A Naxi tribesman, one of Joseph Rock's guides in southwestern China, stands before robes made of leopard skins.**

1916 This Autochrome of the Taj Mahal appeared in a September 1916 *National Geographic* article called "Scenes in Many Lands."

▲ **1927** Circling the Society's headquarters building, a vast crowd clamors for tickets to see Charles Lindbergh receive the Hubbard Medal for his solo crossing of the Atlantic.

In the first decades of the 20th century men and women fanned out to every corner of the globe in cars, airplanes, ships, and on bicycles. Explorers and adventurers made front-page news and were welcomed home with ticker-tape parades. Like baseball players, Robert E. Peary and Ernest Shackleton appeared on trading cards. And the star power of Charles Lindbergh and Amelia Earhart drew thunderous ovations wherever they went.

In spite of the exhilarating pace of exploration in the 1920s, 65 percent of Americans still lived in rural areas,

◀ **1931** Filled with thrilling stories for armchair travelers, *National Geographic* delivered the world to members' doorsteps. October 1931 featured the famous Citroën-Haardt Trans-Asiatic Expedition.

and *National Geographic* provided to its members an important window on the world. As soon as new photographic processes made it possible—and well ahead of other magazines—Gilbert Grosvenor brought color to its pages. His motive was to present reality—to let readers see things as they really were. The world, after all, was in color, not black-and-white.

▲ **1929** Navigating with a compass designed by chief cartographer of the Society Albert H. Bumstead, Richard Byrd and four companions became the first people to fly over the South Pole.

In 1910 *National Geographic* published 24 pages of photographs from Korea and Japan, shot by a wealthy, well-traveled gentleman named William Wisner Chapin. A Japanese artist hand-tinted the pictures in delicate colors. Other tinted pictures followed. Meanwhile, chemists around the world had struggled to develop real color photography. In 1907 the Lumière brothers in France devised the first practical commercial color process, using dyed grains of potato starch on a glass plate. They called it Autochrome. The first natural color photograph to appear in the magazine was an Autochrome published in the July 1914 *Geographic.*

▲ **1910** The November 1910 *Geographic* carried 24 pages of hand-tinted images of Korea and Japan, at the time the largest collection of photographs in color ever published in a magazine.

But Autochromes were expensive and difficult to find. Photographers had to travel with such bulky gear and volatile chemicals that each photograph was nearly as labor-intensive as painting in oils. In 1915 the Geographic hired Franklin Fisher, who established the first color photographic laboratory in American publishing. He recruited a team of artist-technicians who began to systematically show the world in photographic color for the first time. National Geographic photographers would process their Autochrome plates in the field and pack them into padded crates for steamer trips to America. Many contributing photographers never saw the headquarters in Washington throughout their distinguished careers.

▲ **1916** Minute grains of potato starch—dyed green, red, and blue—filtered light and captured the vivid color in this Autochrome of dancers in Indian clothing.

In 1924 Fisher gained his first administrative assistant—Melville Bell Grosvenor, son of the boss, a U.S. Naval Academy graduate just released from a year of active duty with the peacetime Navy. For the next four years, Fisher and young Mel selected all of the pictures published in *National Geographic.* This was the era when even mundane assignments created photographic history. Society records glow with "firsts"—as in the "first natural color photographs of Arctic life," the "first natural color photographs from the air," and the only "natural color photographs of the coronation of Ethiopian emperor Haile Selassie."

One "first" stands out as a true pioneering achievement. In a clear lagoon in Florida's Dry Tortugas, Charles Martin, head of the Geographic's photo lab, and ichthyologist W.H. Longley made the world's first undersea color photographs. Martin constructed a flash-powder mechanism that was synchronized to a submerged camera encased in brass. Longley carried the camera, wearing a bulky diver's helmet with an air hose attached to a compressor on a dory. On the surface, Martin tended a huge reflector and enough magnesium powder to blow up the whole project. The bursts of powder were deafening and blinding, and Longley was seriously burned. Their pictures were published in January 1927.

As membership soared past a million in 1926, National Geographic dispatched "photographic expeditions" to the Caribbean and South America, to western Europe and the Balkans, and to Asia. Professional writers and photographers became the explorers; accurate and penetrating documentation became the science of the expedition.

The story behind getting the story quickly became a beloved tradition among the readers of the *Geographic.* In the caption that accompanied a lively color image of folk dancers in Austria in 1938, W. Robert Moore wrote, "I took potshots standing up and lying on my stomach in the dusty courtyard. Rough boots kicked up dust, dresses and petticoats swished; they were having an altogether good time in a spontaneous dance. So was I."

▾ **1910** Photographer O.D. von Engeln washes his film in seawater among Alaska icebergs.

▾ **1920s–1940s** *National Geographic* photographers carried medium- and large-format cameras like this Graflex Series B.

▲ **1926** Exploding flash powder illuminates the waters around the Dry Tortugas enough to expose the first color photographs (including the hogfish at right) ever made of the undersea world. Ichthyologist W.H. Longley, who collaborated with National Geographic Society laboratory chief Charles Martin on the endeavor, was seriously burned in the process, which required igniting an entire pound of magnesium flash powder to provide enough light to brighten the sea.

Joseph Rock became the first American to visit the Kingdom of Muli in China's Sichuan Province, dispatching a dozen articles to the magazine from remote Asian outposts. Upon his return, he confided to his editor, "my soul still dwells in the great silences among the snow peaks."

In Venezuela and Brazil, Ernest G. Holt made the first systematic collections of birds and animals from areas of South America previously unknown to naturalists. Ranging even farther afield, an NGS–Smithsonian–Yale University expedition to Nepal led by S. Dillon Ripley became the first Western scientific expedition to enter parts of that country in a century. It returned with a trove of specimens, including the spiny babbler, a bird long thought extinct.

In the high peaks of the Yukon, Bradford Washburn and his team embarked on a bold mapping mission by airplane, during which they charted a 5,000-square-mile area in northern Canada that was literally a blank space on the map before they ventured into it.

The venerable staff writer of that era, Frederick Simpich, wrote an amazing 89 stories for the *Geographic*. For decades his craggy, cheerful face made friends over most of the world. His style, too, perfectly mirrored the enthusiasm of Gilbert Grosvenor, who was never satisfied with the verb "to be." He wanted action words and dynamic prose, and Simpich tossed around exclamation marks like confetti. He was hugely popular with readers.

But no one typified the new breed more than Maynard Owen Williams, the Society's first foreign correspondent. A large, gregarious, and enthusiastic man, the former missionary in China and Syria contributed text or photographs, or both, to some 100 articles. Williams was present at the opening of King Tut's tomb, made color photographs of the Arctic, and was the only American selected to join the grandiose, motorized French Citroën-Haardt Expedition across Asia. Near the end of the 314-day, 7,370-mile expedition, temperatures dropped so low that Williams had to suck on his frozen fountain pen to thaw the ink. "Never grieve for me if it is my good fortune to die with my boots on," Williams once wrote to Grosvenor. "That's what I most hope for."

Williams pioneered the Foreign Editorial Staff, a legendary group of correspondents who could both write and photograph stories, often taking two years or more to cover distant parts of the world.

In the 1930s "miniature" 35-mm cameras paired with a dazzling new color film, Kodachrome, to revolutionize the magazine. Luis Marden, a self-educated, multilingual color enthusiast, arrived at the Geographic in 1934 at the age of 21.

▾ **1923** Covering the opening of Tutankhamun's tomb for the magazine, Maynard Owen Williams (below, emerging from King Tut's tomb) wrote, "There is drama in the very air ..."

▾ **1940s** The Society's headquarters as pictured on a 1940s postcard

ON ASSIGNMENT

THE GREATEST JOB IN THE WORLD?

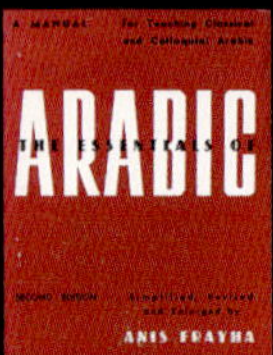

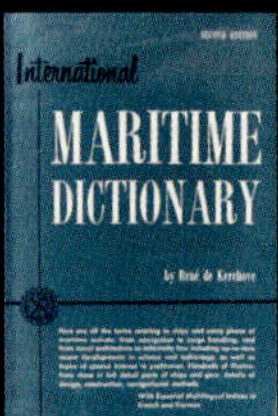

▲ **1960s** Getting along in the field requires ingenuity, good humor, and an occasional phrase of goodwill in Tahitian, Urdu, or Arabic. The dictionaries above were both used on assignment by staffers.

Rain. Camera malfunctions. Ruined film. Vehicle breakdowns. Uncooperative critters. Customs hassles. Interminable waits in train stations, in airports, in offices, for permissions, for interviews. Close encounters with unfriendly stares. Equipment stolen. Too many roaches. Too many mosquitoes. Too many mysterious maladies. Too many bouts of food poisoning. It's too hot. It's too cold. Life in the field can be a lonely and frustrating affair.

So, once again, you make do. You trudge through the rain. You improvise makeshift repairs. You wait for the animals to show. You buy new film and substitute other equipment. You smile and eat it anyway. You put up with reckless drivers, leaky boats, stubborn mules, ill-tempered camels, even yaks, to get where you need to go. You adapt to changing circumstances—if at all possible, with aplomb and savoir faire. Your success demands resourcefulness, patience, good humor, good judgment, street smarts, and a talent for roughing it. So open your eyes, try to have fun, but always gather good material. Make the most of misadventures. If you do, and your work gives rise to a great *Geographic* story, then you can finally relax and admit you have the greatest job in the world. ■

▶ **1940s** Filing from the field, correspondent Howell Walker improvised an office in a remote corner of Australia.

He immediately saw the potential in the new combination. Kodachrome offered the richest color yet, it could be enlarged easily, and its enhanced speed—its ability to gather light—allowed photographers to shoot with small 35-mm cameras. No more tripods and posed pictures; no more glass plates packed into steamer trunks. Action pictures in color were possible for the first time. Melville Grosvenor remembered the heady intoxication: "We just threw out our other pictures from the field—just scrapped them and replaced them as fast as we could with Kodachromes. I'll never forget that—that was really a thrill."

By the 1930s the Society had outgrown Hubbard

▲ **1931** Crossing Asia by pony, camel, yak, and car, Maynard Owen Williams accompanied the Citroën-Haardt Expedition as chief photographer from 1931 to 1932. Though the 18-month journey ended abruptly with Georges-Marie Haardt's death in 1932, Williams called it "the greatest adventure of my life."

▶ **1942** The July 1942 issue carried the first illustration printed on the cover. At the government's request, many American magazines showed the flag and encouraged people to buy savings bonds to support the war effort.

▲ **1937** Kodachrome film freed photographers from the tyranny of posed pictures. This frame by W. Robert Moore captures the whirling action of Burgenland dancers in Austria.

Hall, its original headquarters, and had built a dignified, three-story extension with wood paneling and Italian marble stairs and luxurious fittings. In 1943 the *New Yorker* published a three-part profile of Gilbert Grosvenor that offers a glimpse of what it was like to work at the Society in those days:

The twenty or so editors of the Geographic, *all of them notably polite individuals who are forever bowing to one another through the sculptured bronze doors of their elevators, move in a leisurely welter of thick rugs, bookshelves stocked with encyclopedias, bound volumes of the* Geographic; *interoffice memorandum slips with "Memorandum from Dr. Grosvenor"; incoming correspondence stamped with "Commendation," "Criticism," or "Suggestions." For business errands around*

▶ **1927** In the 1920s the Society commissioned N.C. Wyeth to paint a mural series for the Society depicting the era's ideas of exploration. Several of the images appeared in the magazine in March 1928.

town, the editors have a fleet of five chauffeur-driven cars. They lunch in three private dining rooms, drinking buttermilk, exchanging puns, and ordering excellent à la carte meals from menus on which prices are discreetly omitted.

In reality, the staff was considerably rougher around the edges. But Grosvenor's courtly manner gave the offices of the Geographic an air of refinement.

▲ **1944** During World War II, National Geographic maps were widely used by the military.

When World War II came, the Geographic opened its vast files of photographs, more than 300,000 at that time, to the armed forces. By matching prewar aerial photographs against wartime ones, analysts detected camouflage and gathered intelligence. One high-ranking general wrote to Gilbert Grosvenor in 1946 that the Geographic files "proved to be the richest and most helpful single source of pictorial material" that the armed forces had.

With the wartime boost, photographic technology was exploding. Harold E. "Doc" Edgerton, a professor at Massachusetts Institute of Technology, had developed the high-speed electronic flash in 1931 and perfected it with the help of National Geographic grants. From the late 1940s through the 1970s, Edgerton was a contributor to the magazine with such mind-boggling images as a bullet frozen in the act of bursting through an apple.

▲ **1944** Gen. Dwight D. Eisenhower uses a National Geographic map of Germany. Red Cross workers used Society maps to locate Japanese POW camps, and Army engineers posted the Germany map at many European intersections.

National Geographic sponsored more than 100 expeditions from the 1920s through the 1950s. Exploration in these decades sought to probe the planet's physical extremes—from pole to pole, from the tallest peaks to the deepest ocean trenches. The June 1931 *National Geographic* published William Beebe's account of climbing with Otis Barton into a steel bathysphere off Bermuda and plunging—deeper than any person before

▸ **1964** Frozen in time, this image of a bullet shooting through an apple was captured with stroboscopic photography invented by grantee Harold "Doc" Edgerton. In the 1950s Edgerton and Jacques-Yves Cousteau worked together to advance underwater photography.

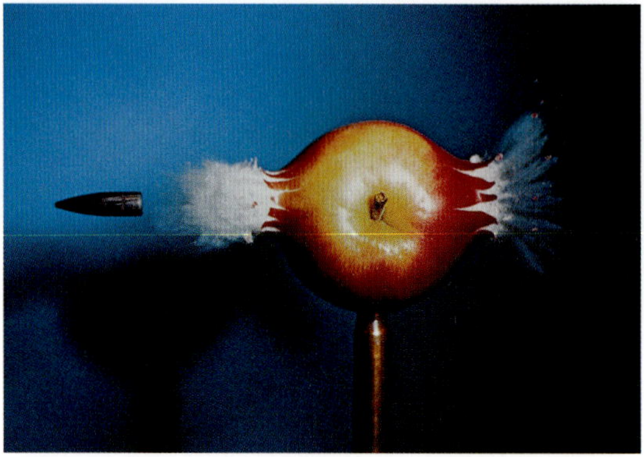

▾ **1934** William Beebe emerges from the bathysphere that took him and Otis Barton on a record dive a half mile below the surface of the sea.

them—into inky darkness. Tethered to a barge on the surface, the capsule bounced like a yo-yo as it drifted past transparent fish and pale shrimps, "ghostly things in every direction," wrote Beebe. In 1934, under Geographic sponsorship, Beebe and Barton descended nearly twice as deep, to 3,028 feet, a record that stood for the next 15 years.

The March 1933 *Geographic* carried the accounts of balloonist Auguste Piccard's record-breaking ascents to altitudes higher than 53,000 feet, more than 10 miles, in hydrogen-filled balloons. "The stratosphere is the superhighway of future intercontinental transport," Piccard predicted. A year later National Geographic joined the U.S. Army Air Corps to sponsor the *Explorer I* stratospheric balloon flight. Albert W. Stevens, William Kepner, and Orvil Anderson climbed into a round gondola, outfitted with four tons of scientific equipment. For protection, the men wore football helmets borrowed from a local high school.

The trio was already past record heights at 60,000 feet when they heard a fearsome clatter. Wrote Stevens, "We were startled to see a large rip in the balloon's lower surface ... Through the overhead glass

◀ **1934** Just over a year after Maj. William Kepner (left) kicked Capt. Albert W. Stevens free of the plummeting *Explorer I*, Stevens and Capt. Orvil Anderson reached the stratosphere and a record altitude of 13.71 miles in *Explorer II* (below) on November 11, 1935. The balloon record held for 21 years.

porthole we watched the rent in the fabric gradually become larger and larger." Suddenly the bottom of the balloon dropped out, the gondola plunged into free fall, and the men struggled to bail out with their parachutes. Anderson catapulted off into space, but Stevens got stuck halfway through the small hatch of the gondola. Kepner kicked furiously at Stevens's chest to push him out. They were only 300 feet from Earth when they tumbled free and pulled their rip cords. The capsule then crashed into a Nebraska cornfield. Undeterred, Stevens and Anderson lifted off in *Explorer II* only 16 months later and set a balloon altitude record of 72,395 feet that stood for the next 21 years.

Perhaps nothing so exemplified the venturesome spirit of the Geographic as did Luis Marden's quest for the famous ship H.M.S. *Bounty*. Everyone knew that *Bounty* had been sailed by her mutinous crew to Pitcairn Island, a lonely speck in the vast Pacific,

WHAT LIES BENEATH

ARCHAEOLOGY AT NATIONAL GEOGRAPHIC

▼ **1930s** Clearing debris from a colossal 2,300-year-old stone head, archaeologist Matthew Stirling probes the ruins of the Olmec, an early Mexican civilization. His expedition battled dense jungle and intense heat to reach the ancient ruins.

▶ **1920s** An exquisite beaded turquoise necklace (right) and striking pottery (opposite page) from New Mexico's Chaco Canyon provide clues about a culture that existed there 1,000 years ago.

Since the dawn of civilization humans have left fragments of their existence for later generations to uncover and interpret. And while rarely are the finds as exciting as a lost city or a mummy, one of the Society's areas of focus has always been human histories and cultures, supporting Explorers in fields such as archaeology and paleoanthropology.

The first archaeological expedition sponsored by the Geographic did cause excitement. In 1913 Hiram Bingham reported in *National Geographic* the existence of Machu Picchu, an Inca citadel high in the Peruvian Andes. This was followed by the work of Neil Judd, who in the 1920s explored Pueblo Bonito, or "beautiful village," situated in present-day New Mexico's Chaco Canyon National Historical Park. And in the forests of Mexico in the 1930s Matthew Stirling found traces of the Olmec, a civilization whose colossal stone heads, jade necklaces, and mysterious objects are not yet fully understood. Society-supported archaeologists have found royal Moche tombs in Peru, the frozen mummy of the "Inca Ice Maiden," and a staircase covered with hieroglyphs in Honduras. Farther north, in L'Anse aux Meadows, Newfoundland, Helge Ingstad uncovered proof that Norsemen had visited the New World five centuries prior to Columbus, while in Virginia, William Kelso excavated the site of James Fort at Jamestown.

And Egypt, land of the pharaohs, never fails to deliver spectacular reve-

◂ **1964** Carefully, a worker delivers a reconstructed pot to waiting hands at Mesa Verde, an ancestral Puebloan site in Colorado. Archaeologists employed a variety of scientific techniques, including tree-ring dating and studying ancient insects, to piece together life at the site in the 1300s.

▴ **1978** This Thracian battle helmet, excavated in Bulgaria, dates from the sixth century B.C.E.

lations. Maynard Owen Williams recorded the breathless opening of Tutankhamun's tomb in 1922. Since then the Society has supported the video camera "excavation" of a pharaonic boat near the Pyramids at Giza in the late 1980s and Explorer Francesco Porcelli's comprehensive scan of King Tut's tomb with ground-penetrating radar in 2018 (no secret chambers containing Nefertiti's remains were found).

These fragments of history are part of our ever expanding human story, one that continues to promise great wonders and puzzles for those who seek it out. ■

▸ **1957** Fletcher Christian, great-great-grandson of a famous mutineer, negotiates the recovery of the anchor from the H.M.S. *Bounty* at Pitcairn Island.

and burned and sunk there in 1790. No one, however, had thought to seek her remains until Luis Marden, on a whim, decided to cross half the globe to find them. Finally arriving at Pitcairn in December 1956, Marden, an early disciple of scuba diving, spent weeks searching fruitlessly in the pounding surf and dangerous currents. Then, in January 1957, near the end of his stay, he spotted an oarlock on the sea bottom, and then a long sandy trench full of what looked like petrified worms—copper sheathing nails marking the former keel of a ship. The wood had long since disappeared, but other bits of hull fittings were nearby.

So was the anchor. They were all that remained of *Bounty,* but they were pieces of a legend.

Marden cabled back to Society headquarters the cryptic message: "Have found the curlew's nest," so that the news services would not scoop the story. In December 1957 "I Found the Bones of the *Bounty*" was published in *National Geographic* magazine; it caused an international sensation. Even the motion picture Marden had made was in demand—so much so that it became the first Society film ever broadcast on television.

▲ **1959** A diver recovers a 1,000-year-old Maya jar from a cenote (natural well) in Dzibilchaltún, Mexico, a site excavated by E. Wyllys Andrews of Tulane University.

In 1954 Gilbert H. Grosvenor, the "geographer to millions," retired at the age of 78, passing on the editorship to his longtime associate John Oliver La Gorce. Grosvenor had made the Society and its magazine a national institution, but times were changing, and the institution would need to change with them. La Gorce was a caretaker, really, in preparation for the time that Melville Grosvenor "inherited" the office.

The Geographic was not a family-owned business, but neither was it a corporation, and the Board of Trustees was simply acknowledging the talent and leadership of the Grosvenor family. Melville—imbued with his grandfather Bell's insatiable curiosity, his father's common touch, and his mother's charm—would be the one who broadened the Society's activities and modernized its magazine in a decade-long expansion.

When Melville became Editor on January 8, 1957, he embraced change

LUIS MARDEN

Once described as the epitome of the Geographic man, Luis Marden (1913–2003) was a self-taught scholar, linguist, botanist, navigator, diver, and pilot who pioneered the Society's use of 35-mm color photography. An enthusiastic traveler, Marden roamed most of the world in his more than 40 years as a writer and photographer for the Society.

▲ **1963** Born in a three-week frenzy of activity that produced a guide to Jacqueline Kennedy's refurbished White House, the Special Publications division quickly became an important part of the Society. Melville Grosvenor (above right) presents the finished product on July 4, 1963. One of its editors, Robert L. Breeden, would over the next two decades turn such incipient efforts into an astonishingly successful publishing endeavor that has sold millions of books.

and innovation so that the Society might widen its scope and appeal. Although to some conservative members it verged on sacrilege, in 1959 Melville slapped color pictures on magazine covers that had traditionally been mere tables of contents, framed by a border of oak and laurel leaves. He had an even more ambitious goal: full color in the magazine. When the February 1962 *National Geographic* came off the Society's new state-of-the-art printing presses, there was not a single black-and-white picture in it. The *Geographic* was the first periodical in the U.S. to achieve this technological milestone.

Aware that the Society was regarded as a national institution, Melville emphasized public service as a Society responsibility. First Lady Jacqueline Kennedy was so impressed by a *National Geographic* article on the White House that she persuaded the White House Historical Association to ask the Society to produce an official guidebook to the executive mansion. That request could be accommo-

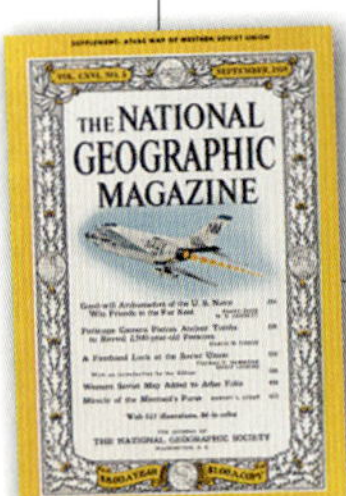

◂ **1959** Believing photographs on the cover would help identify each issue, Melville Bell Grosvenor broke new ground in September 1959. Irate members complained but soon learned to love the cover photographs.

◀ **1958** A girl gazes at a picturesque Belgian scene in this photo. Placing brightly clad people to set off beautiful scenery maximized the capabilities of Kodachrome photography in the 1950s and came to be playfully known as the "red shirt" school of photography.

dated because the Society had recently launched a new book publishing arm, the Book Service, which complemented the magazine and fed readers' continued hunger for captivating stories and photography.

A soaring new 10-story marble headquarters next to the original building, on the corner of 17th and M Streets in Washington, D.C., was built to hold the growing Society. Explorers Hall, a museum and exhibition space, dominated the ground floor and featured an 11-foot-wide revolving globe. President Lyndon B. Johnson dedicated the new headquarters in 1964, remarking that the "Society had broadened the horizons and narrowed the misunderstandings of many generations."

These were exciting years for the National Geographic Society. But on February 4, 1966, Gilbert Hovey Grosvenor died at the age of 90. In 1957 he had written about his lifelong labor of love: "But not for youth itself would I trade the treasures stored in my memory: The rich experiences of one who roamed always with a hungry heart, the friendships I have enjoyed with men and women of courage and destiny, and, above all, the immeasurable satisfaction of seeing the National Geographic Society and its magazine surpass my every dream." ■

▼ **1949** The Grosvenor Medal—named for Gilbert H. Grosvenor—is awarded for outstanding contributions to geography. It is one of several medals bestowed by the Society for extending the boundaries of exploration and discovery.

DID YOU WATCH THE GEOGRAPHIC LAST NIGHT?

"Challenge and inspiration are the greatest treasures from the sea. We are just beginning to learn her science, art, and philosophy and how to live in her embrace."

JACQUES-YVES COUSTEAU

◂ 1960s A filmmaker treads gingerly along a glacial deposit to shoot footage for one of the Society's first Television Specials, *Alaska!*, which aired on CBS in 1967. National Geographic Television Specials heralded the dawn of a new era for the Society. By the end of the 1960s the Specials had become highly anticipated events.

1965 In Tanzania's Gombe Stream National Park, chimpanzees groom themselves unselfconsciously as Jane Goodall notes their behavior.

▲ **1963** Pushing toward the summit of Everest, climbers use steel boot spikes to hold their footing on the steep slopes. The first successful expedition of Americans to Mount Everest was sponsored in part by the Society.

In 1963 the National Geographic Society reached the top of the world. On May 22 Barry Bishop of the magazine staff planted the Society's flag on the summit of Mount Everest. Bishop was a member of the first American team—and one of the first groups—to summit the world's tallest mountain. His feat crowned the Society's 75th anniversary. For three-quarters of a century the Geographic had grown ever larger until its membership now topped three million. As its staff prepared to move into the new marble headquarters building, the Society released its first world atlas, long dreamed of and seven years in the actual making. Melville Grosvenor deemed it the Society's

◀ **1966** When the famous onion domes of Moscow's St. Basil's Cathedral appeared on the March 1966 cover, they announced that the magazine was tackling a once taboo subject: the Soviet Union.

"largest, handsomest and most ambitious contribution to Geographic knowledge." Never in history had so many opportunities beckoned. President John F. Kennedy had promised to explore the stars and tap the ocean depths. Science and exploration were expanding at a rapid pace—and the National Geographic Society looked for new ways to bring the world to its readers. Photographic and printing innovations allowed *National Geographic* to explode with color. Whatever the subject—the Italian Riviera, New Guinea, hummingbirds, or sleek jet aircraft—it was presented in dynamic new layouts. Vivid illustrations splashed across the cover. Melville Grosvenor tripled the photographic budget and hired a bright new staff of photographers and writers with fresh ideas.

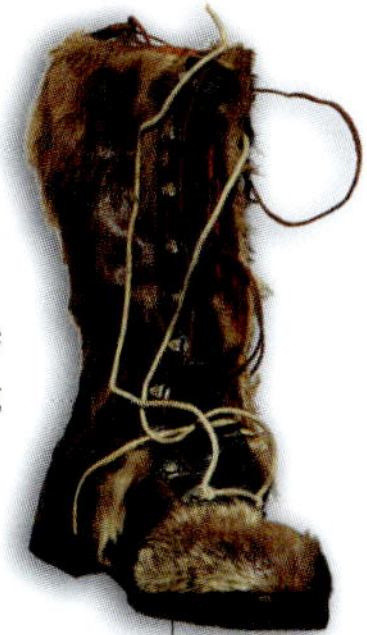

▲ **1963** Leather-and-fur boots worn by Barry Bishop for the 1963 ascent of Mount Everest

Nor was that all. The Society's lecture program, featuring narrated films, had long been a popular Washington institution. But Grosvenor saw in the advent of color television the perfect platform for carrying such films to the nation at large. On September 10, 1965, the Society aired its first Television Special. *Americans on Everest* made an astonishing impact, receiving the highest ratings of any documentary broadcast to that time. Soon four Specials a year were not only elevating the standards of the format but they also were regularly attracting large audiences. By 1968, when *Amazon* aired, it drew 35 million viewers, more than any other show on television in a two-week period.

▲ **1959** Densely packed color and dynamic layouts on almost every page showcased the power of color photography in the 1950s and '60s.

The Geographic's heroes of old had been intrepid explorers and frostbitten gentlemen framed in the magazine's oak and laurel. But such Television Specials as *Miss Goodall and the*

▲ **1959** Jacques-Yves Cousteau received 37 grants from the Society. A staff artist commemorated one of his visits with the caricature at right, drawn in the Society's official guest book.

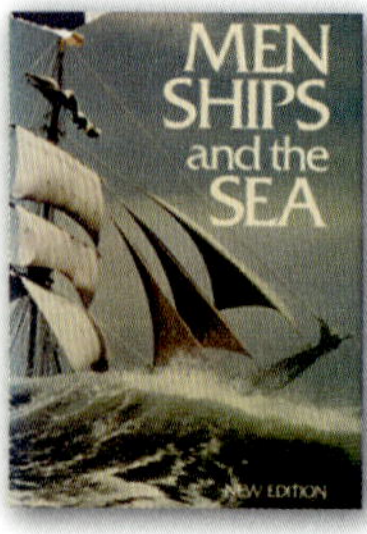

▲ **1962** *Men, Ships, and the Sea* by Alan Villiers chronicled the history of sailing.

Wild Chimpanzees, Dr. Leakey and the Dawn of Man, and *The World of Jacques-Yves Cousteau* brought new heroes, emerging from specialized fields of science, into every living room.

Few captured the popular imagination as did Frenchman Jacques-Yves Cousteau. Charismatic and visionary, Cousteau had co-developed the Aqua-Lung, the first true underwater breathing device, which opened up a whole new realm for exploration. But he was little known outside France until the Geographic in 1952 began sponsoring his projects. Working from his famous research vessel, *Calypso,* Cousteau then pioneered new underwater filming techniques with strobe inventor Harold Edgerton. He developed a rudderless diving saucer that could maneuver with

thruster nozzles like an underwater airplane. He built a series of undersea dwellings named Conshelf, proving that humans could live and work for long periods beneath the waves. Over the years he took readers with him through a dozen popular articles in *National Geographic*. And the success of the Society's 1966 Television Special eventually led Cousteau to develop his own long-running television series.

▾ **1960s** Using the grid techniques of classical archaeology, George Bass almost single-handedly pioneered the science of underwater archaeology.

The Aqua-Lung had permitted archaeologist George Bass of the University of Pennsylvania to systematically excavate—on the seabed—both Bronze Age and Byzantine-era shipwrecks, lying deep off the coast of southern Turkey. Supported by the Society, Bass pioneered the science of underwater archaeology and would eventually contribute a half dozen accounts of his work to *National Geographic*.

In 1959 the Society began sponsoring the work of Louis and Mary Leakey, who had long been probing Tanzania's Olduvai Gorge for traces of human origins. Their discovery of the fossil remains of a 1.8-million-year-old hominin had opened up tremendous new vistas in paleoanthropology. Digging in the exposed cliffs of the eroded gorge the couple collected bone fragments, stone tools, and bits of extinct animals pointing to Africa as the likely cradle of humankind. Louis, with his tousled white hair and mischievous grin, was made familiar to millions through *National Geographic* articles and the Society's 1966 Television Special.

Louis Leakey believed he could gain insight into early humans by studying the great apes. He encouraged a trio of fascinating and courageous

▾ **1960s** A longtime Society grantee, Bass reported on his Byzantine-era shipwreck excavation that yielded this earthenware plate and cup for the July 1963 *Geographic*.

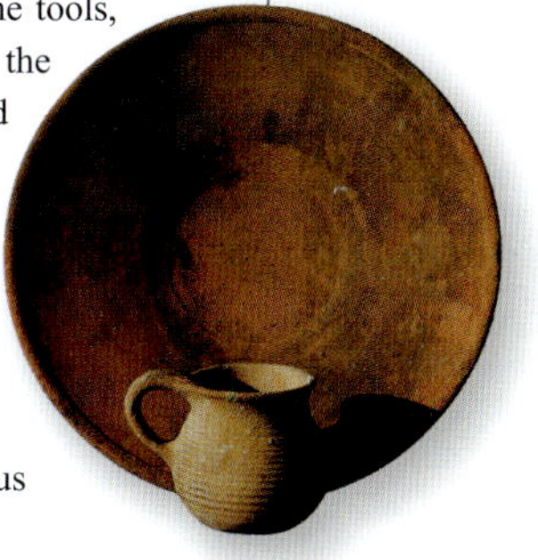

▲ **1961** Louis and Mary Leakey and son Philip examine a 1.7-million-year-old campsite in Tanzania's Olduvai Gorge. The "first family of paleoanthropology," the Leakeys—three generations of them—have also excavated fossils from Kenya's Lake Turkana region. Their work was pivotal in proving Africa to be the cradle of humanity.

▶ **1968** Flo, matriarch of one of Gombe's chimpanzee clans, cradles daughter Flame while son Flint exhibits what appears to be a recognizably human emotion: jealousy.

women to dedicate their careers to primates. Jane Goodall, a soft-spoken young Englishwoman, lived with the chimpanzees frequenting Tanzania's Gombe Stream National Park. There she made the surprising discovery that chimps often fashioned simple tools. Goodall's long relationship with the Society led to numerous articles and Television Specials.

The second researcher, Dian Fossey, left the U.S. in 1967 with a grant from the Society to study mountain gorillas. In the remote Rwandan forests, she soon made observations revealing that gorillas were not ferocious apes but rather shy and gentle creatures. She fiercely protected them from poaching but often used controversial tactics that harmed local people.

Fossey was murdered in 1985. Meanwhile, in the rainforests of Borneo, Biruté Galdikas had embarked in 1971 on a study of orangutans, which the Society supported for many years.

Closer to home, twin brothers Frank and John Craighead advanced wildlife biology by developing radio-tracking devices for large animals. In the August 1960 *National Geographic* they described their efforts, undertaken with Society support, to immobilize Yellowstone grizzly bears with anesthetic darts to safely measure, weigh, and study the powerful animals. Soon they began fitting them with radio-transmitting collars, tracking the bears' wanderings and monitoring their physiology not only via handheld receivers but also eventually by satellite—gaining a better understanding of grizzly habits and behavior. The exciting moments in this work were vividly captured in a 1967 Television Special. These techniques have since become important tools in wildlife studies, used around the globe to study animals from elephants to whales to bats.

The Society had never failed to endorse the preservation of wilderness and natural beauty. The July 1966 *National Geographic* commemorated the 50th anniversary of the National Park Service by showcasing the existing 32 parks. It also urged the creation of a new one. California's magnificent coastal redwood groves were threatened with logging. A Society grant had enabled the Park Service to determine an area that should be safeguarded. A Society team subsequently found in that area what was then the world's tallest tree at more than 367 feet. The July 1966 issue asked Congress to preserve the forests. "Today … redwoods make a last stand

ALL IN THE FAMILY

Under the blazing African sun, three generations of Leakeys have studied the fossils of early humans. Louis S.B. Leakey, a maverick thinker, encountered scorn from mainstream paleoanthropologists in the 1950s when he first insisted that Africa, not Asia, was the cradle of humankind. But at Olduvai Gorge in 1959, Louis's wife, Mary, discovered a 1.8-million-year-old skull (left) that was the oldest hominin fossil then found. More discoveries soon followed, including 3.6-million-year-old hominin footprints left in hardened lava at nearby Laetoli. Continuing the family business, their son Richard and his wife, Meave, led numerous fossil-finding expeditions around Kenya's Lake Turkana, where the camp at Koobi Fora is now directed by their daughter Louise, a National Geographic Explorer at Large.

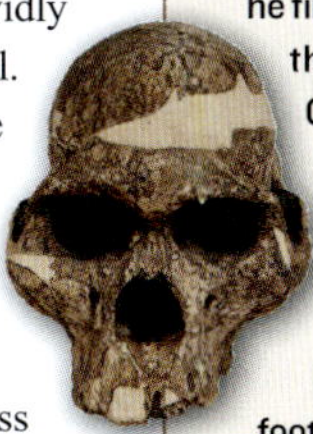

NATIONAL PARKS

A TRADITION OF CONSERVATION

▸ **1925** A fantastic vista of stalagmites dominates the bizarre underworld of New Mexico's Carlsbad Caverns.

▾ **1915** Joined in a protective circle, a party rings a California giant sequoia. National Geographic has long worked to protect natural treasures.

Legend has it that a visiting Englishman once described the national parks as "the best idea America ever had." The National Geographic Society has certainly thought it a good enough idea that for most of its history it has been showcasing the parks through words and pictures, books, magazine articles, maps, and films. Society leaders helped organize the National Park Service, and Society efforts have saved endangered tracts of Sequoia National Park and helped establish Redwood and Shenandoah National Parks.

National Geographic Society field expeditions have explored, mapped, and photographed many areas of sublime scenery that, brought to the world's attention through the magazine, were also considered worthy of incorporation into the park system. That's how the spectacular Valley of Ten Thousand Smokes in Alaska became part of Katmai National Monument, and how an extraordinary cave system in New Mexico was designated Carlsbad Caverns National Park. In the 1950s Society-supported archaeologists excavated 1,500-year-old Native American artifacts from a cave in Alabama. It duly became Russell Cave National Monument. And elsewhere in the world, the creation of Gombe Stream National Park in Tanzania and Gabon's national park system was championed by Society-supported research projects. ■

against the inroads of man," wrote Melville Bell Grosvenor. Such efforts proved fruitful: In 1968 Redwood National Park was officially established.

A startled nation awoke to the space age when the Soviet Union launched the Sputnik satellite in 1957. Even before President Kennedy vowed to put an astronaut on the moon by the end of the decade, *National Geographic* had loaned staff photographer Dean Conger to NASA to make a permanent color record of the crewed space program. Conger's pictures of astronaut Alan Shepard, the first American in space, being plucked from the ocean appeared in newspapers around the world. When in 1962 John Glenn became the first American to orbit Earth, he carried a tiny Geographic flag, and *National Geographic* photographers made historic photos of the launch and recovery.

▲ **1960** Brothers Frank and John Craighead employed innovative techniques in radio tracking, particularly with grizzly bears. Passionate defenders of wildlife, they wrote, "Restoring and maintaining a healthy world ecology depends on man's ability to understand and to respect nature in all her diversity." Animal tagging practices have evolved even further since then.

▸ **2006** The January 2006 cover story of *National Geographic* added depth to readers' understanding of the Grand Canyon, where for "10,000 years people lived, loved, traded, even farmed"—until it was made into a park.

Neil Armstrong also carried a small National Geographic flag when in July 1969 he became the first person to step on the surface of the moon. In December of that year, the magazine published a five-part package on the feat, not only printing the historic words and photographs of the mission but also including a small phonographic record, *Sounds of the Space Age*. Ken Weaver, science editor at the time, wrote, "No one who sat that July night welded to his TV screen will ever forget the sight of that ghostly foot groping slowly past the ladder to *Eagle*'s footpad, and then stepping tentatively onto the virgin soil."

▲ **1969** In one of its most challenging cartographic accomplishments, the Society's "Map of the Moon," published in the February 1969 *National Geographic*, was the first popular map to show the entire lunar surface, including its mysterious far side, on a single sheet.

▶ **1961** Having just completed the first spaceflight made by an American, astronaut Alan Shepard is pulled from the Atlantic into a Navy helicopter. Photographer Dean Conger mounted a camera above the helicopter door that, firing repeatedly, happened to make this stunning shot. Striving to document this most enthralling of adventures, Society photographers like Conger, Luis Marden, and Otis Imboden shared their unrivaled expertise in color photography with both astronauts and NASA technicians.

Beyond the moon the planets beckoned, and beyond the planets, the Milky Way galaxy. Into those great unexplored regions NASA hurled its instrument-laden probes. Soon the faces of Mercury, Venus, and Mars—once known only as stars in the sky—were seen up close in the pages of *National Geographic*. The Society, using data relayed from the probes, produced a map of Mars in 1973, and published historic photos of the Martian surface made by the Viking spacecraft in 1976.

NASA launched two Voyager spacecraft in 1977 that transmitted millions of images of Jupiter, Saturn, and Uranus. Aboard each vessel was a gold-plated record containing sounds and scenes of Earth, encoded as digital pulses. Intermingled with strains of Bach, Mozart, and Louis Armstrong, with the cry of a chimpanzee and the song of a humpback whale, were 16 images provided by the National Geographic Society—including snowflakes, a Balinese dancer, cresting dolphins, the Great Wall of China—images diffusing geographic knowledge to the cosmos.

Science holds a particular fascination for readers, and *National Geographic* earned a reputation for clear presentation of complex topics and difficult subjects in an easily accessible manner, fully illustrated with diagrams and maps. "You and the Obedient Atom," a 1958 article, demonstrated that the atomic age need not be associated only with mushroom clouds but

▲ **1949** Astronomer Edwin Hubble championed what became the National Geographic–Palomar Observatory Sky Survey (1949–1956), a colossal photomapping of the night sky from the Northern Hemisphere, which made an enormous contribution to 20th-century astronomy.

◀ **1961** Astronaut Alan Shepard (left) and photographer Dean Conger share a friendly chat.

might also bring immense benefits to everyday life. "The Laser's Bright Magic," a 1966 story, graphically depicted the nature and potential of that "sword of light." Readers quickly came to rely on the *Geographic*'s science coverage for information about the latest technologies.

In 1957 the International Geophysical Year (IGY) began, a program of worldwide studies embracing land, sea, and sky in an effort to learn more about Earth as a single functioning system. Many countries were involved, and Lyman J. Briggs, chairman of the Society's Research Committee, was a key member of the U.S. organizing committee. Nearly a dozen articles in *National Geographic* profiled various aspects of the program. A number of Society-funded research projects had specific IGY applications, especially the cosmic ray investigations conducted by Martin Pomerantz.

▲ **1979** Voyager I approaching Jupiter

▶ **1966** Lasers transform the Lincoln Memorial in Washington, D.C., into a hologram.

▼ **1930s–1960s** This Leica and other 35-mm range-finder cameras were favorites with photographers between the late 1930s and early 1960s.

Melville also modernized the Society's mapmaking efforts. He soon had the cartographic division laboring away on the first *National Geographic Atlas of the World,* published in 1963. And if he was going to compile an atlas, Melville concluded he might as well produce a globe, too, calling

◂ **1968** Photographer and assistant editor Bill Garrett accompanied the Fifth Marine Battalion as it worked its way through Vietnam's mud and jungle vegetation. It took three hours to travel a third of a mile. One soldier dropped from exhaustion; another was bitten by a venomous snake.

for one that could be freely rotated in its cradle. It would also be capped by a transparent plastic "geometer"—a device that allowed users to trace satellite orbits, calculate azimuths, or solve a host of arcane geographic puzzles. The bells and whistles made it a "globe for the space age," as its designers were calling it. The Smithsonian Institution's Astrophysical Observatory adopted it immediately for use in its satellite tracking stations. But when the finished product was presented to President Kennedy, the geometer slipped off and shattered on the floor.

National Geographic did not shrink from covering such complex subjects as the war in Vietnam. Wilbur E. (Bill) Garrett, a dynamic picture editor from Missouri, shot gritty photographs of that conflict, which continued pushing a harder-hitting photojournalism into the magazine's once staid pages. Staff writer Peter White's reports ranged from Saigon to the Mekong Delta to villages and rice paddies. Staff photographer Emory Kristof caught a mortar fragment in his eye while covering a Thanksgiving Day patrol.

▾ **1973** Exploring a giant cleft in the sheer face of the Greek island of Cephalonia

BECAUSE IT IS THERE

MOUNTAINEERING AT THE GEOGRAPHIC

▲ **1966** Nicholas Clinch battles his way to the summit of Vinson Massif, Antarctica's highest peak. Clinch led National Geographic's American Antarctic Expedition, which became the first to climb the continent's highest peaks, located in the Sentinel Range of the Ellsworth Mountains.

"Why?" The question was asked of George Mallory when he sought to become the first person to climb Mount Everest. His answer—"Because it is there"—is a poignant expression of the irresistible lure of mountains, which has played a major role in the Society's history.

Though Israel Russell did not reach the summit of Mount St. Elias on the Society's first expedition in 1890, his thrilling account of the attempt filled the May 1891 issue of the magazine. Mountaineering, essential to determining the geography of many unknown places, was an important component of subsequent expeditions, including Robert Griggs's expedition to Alaska's Valley of Ten Thousand Smokes, where he achieved the first summit of Mount Katmai.

Mountaineering legend Bradford Washburn led a 1935 Society expedition to the Yukon in which he mapped more than 5,000 square miles of territory previously marked "unknown" on the map. Washburn and his wife, Barbara, circled the globe, completing the most detailed maps of the Grand Canyon and Mount Everest ever created. In 1998, at age 88, Washburn directed the efforts of a team that used GPS to calculate the precise height of Everest, adding seven feet to the world's tallest mountain.

The Society awarded Edmund Hillary and Tenzing Norgay the Hubbard Medal for making the first ascent of Everest in 1953. Ten years later the Society helped sponsor the first American expedition to the summit. In 1978 the *Geographic* published Reinhold Messner's account of the first ascent of Everest without oxygen. Messner went on to climb all 14 of the world's 8,000-meter peaks without oxygen. Society grantee Ed Viesturs, the first American to match Messner's feat, aided in the rescue effort for the climbers lost on Everest in 1996, a tragedy documented in the book *Into Thin Air*.

In 2019 the Society sponsored the largest scientific expedition ever attempted on Mount Everest. The members of the National Geographic and Rolex Perpetual Planet Everest Expedition—experts in glaciology, geology, meteorology, biology, and mapping—installed five weather stations on the world's tallest mountain to give scientists unprecedented data on climate change. Their hope? To "turn the science into something that has value to the people" who live in Everest's shadow. ■

▲ **1941** Barbara and Brad Washburn stand atop Alaska's Mount Hayes.

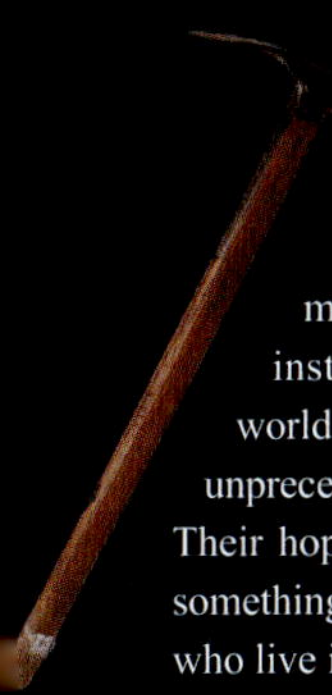

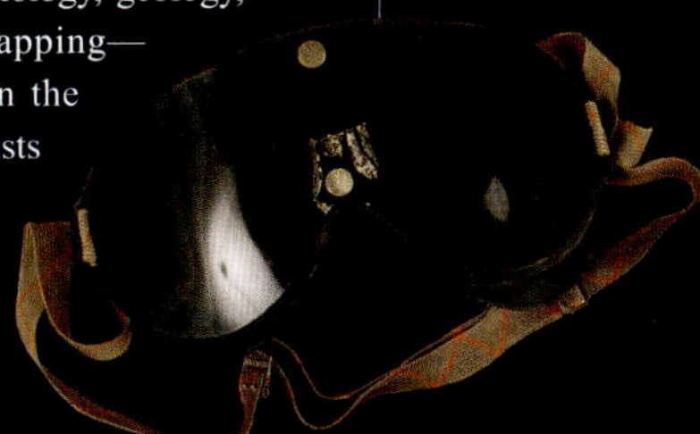

▼ **1963** A pair of protective goggles and an ice pick (at left), important tools of the mountaineer's trade

▲ **1966** "Like a vision from the heroic days of sail, she rose up from the dark-blue shield of the Pacific ..." The brigantine *Yankee,* described by Luis Marden, made globe-girdling voyages with crews of young adults.

And freelance photographer Dickey Chapelle contributed pictures and stories before becoming the first American female correspondent killed in action.

Science and photojournalism notwithstanding, *National Geographic* always reserved room for starry-eyed adventurers. Among them was Melville Bell Grosvenor himself, who above all else loved to rove the sea. His own articles describing voyages in his yacht, *White Mist,* were enormously popular. So were those of the great

◀ **1969** Marking the apogee of human exploration, the December 1969 *National Geographic* featured five different articles about the historic moon landing and included a record, *Sounds of the Space Age.*

sailor Alan Villiers. He capped off his Geographic contributions with the best-selling book *Men, Ships, and the Sea,* filled with tales of Magellan, Drake, and other great seafarers. Year in and year out, Irving Johnson sailed his storied *Yankee* all over the globe, and readers of the magazine followed his adventures. If they also watched the 1966 Television Special *Voyage of the Brigantine Yankee,* they heard for the first time the trumpet fanfare that would become the Geographic's television signature.

But no one seemed to captivate readers as did an adventurous schoolboy, Robin Lee Graham, who sailed alone out of Los Angeles one July day in 1965 in a 24-foot fiberglass sloop named *Dove*. When he returned, 1,739 days and 30,000 nautical miles later, he had a new wife, a new sloop, and legions of admiring fans enthralled by his three *National Geographic* articles. "Why did I choose to sail around the world?" Graham wrote. "I want to see the world, and not on a tourist's itinerary with a passport stamped full of one-day visas. No, my passport must be imprinted with memories of landfalls where foreigners seldom set foot."

By the time of his retirement, Melville Bell Grosvenor had steered the National Geographic Society in many new directions. Its magazines, books, and television programs were reaching out in new ways to new audiences while retaining that glorious photography and distinctive style of storytelling. ■

▾ **1968** Robin Lee Graham charts his solo course around the world.

▾ **1959** Melville Bell Grosvenor, President and Editor of the National Geographic Society between 1957 and 1967, at Angkor Wat

LIVING WITH THE PLANET

"More and more people are opening their hearts to the desperation they see around them and springing into action. For this is how we can attain our human potential for compassion. And for love."

JANE GOODALL

◂ **1977 Digit, a Rwandan mountain gorilla studied by Dian Fossey, a National Geographic Society grantee and protégée of Louis Leakey. Fossey did much to dispel myths about the ferocious nature of these creatures. Digit was killed by poachers.**

1981 The stump of Mount St. Helens still smolders nearly a year after its May 18, 1980, eruption. The January 1981 *National Geographic* article on the cataclysm became one of the most popular stories in the magazine's history.

▲ **1977** Sunlight filters through a fragile Eden of ancient trees in California's Redwood National Park. Some of the trees are more than 400 years old and stand taller than the Statue of Liberty.

When Gil Grosvenor, grandson of former Editor in Chief Gilbert Grosvenor, became the Editor of *National Geographic* in 1970, he announced that the magazine would thenceforth serve as "a mirror of its times, reflecting the changes through which we pass." And the times were changing. Setting the tone of the new era, a visually uncompromising article on pollution was the cover story of the December 1970 issue. Over the next few years, articles on Castro's Cuba and South African apartheid entered the magazine's editorial mix. And still, *National Geographic* magazine, maps, books, lectures, and television programs were reaching an audience of millions.

One of the biggest changes came from a powerful

◂ **1970** Environmental issues took center stage in the December 1970 issue of *National Geographic,* which featured extended coverage of "Our Ecological Crisis."

new force sweeping the nation: the environmental movement. The *Geographic* had always addressed natural history subjects. Birds had long been a popular staple, as were articles by Paul Zahl, staff naturalist, who took his family with him in a succession of wood-paneled station wagons in quest of natural curiosities. But now the magazine was suffused by this emerging environmental consciousness. The *Geographic* showcased the vanishing wildlife of Africa and Asia. It highlighted the plight of elephants, pandas, rhinoceroses, and whales. It summarized the challenges of pesticides, nuclear power, and acid rain. In 1981 an extra—a 13th issue, devoted to the topic of energy—was so well received that 50,000 additional copies had to be printed to meet press and government requests. Aiming for impartiality, the magazine offered all sides of complex technological and ecological issues. *National Geographic* was presenting readers the same beautiful world but seen in another light.

Meanwhile, other Society branches also budded in new directions. Educational and book publishing flourished. Maps broadened their scope to include relevant cultural and historical information. And in 1975, the Society launched *World* magazine for eight- to 14-year-olds, which soon was reaching 1.3 million youngsters.

Society-supported scientists in the field were also seeking to understand this changing world. Biologists studied not only animals but also their rapidly disappearing habitats. George

▲ **1970** A three-page foldout of Ohio's devastated Cuyahoga River in the December issue epitomizes the magazine's new direction. In 1969 the river had become so polluted with oil that it actually caught fire, destroying two railroad bridges.

▲ **1970s** The Nikon 35-mm single-lens reflex was the camera of choice by the 1970s. Digital SLRs are photojournalists' preferred tools today.

▲ **1970s–1980s**
Photojournalists spread out across the globe, shooting fraught scenes such as the 1973 eruption of Iceland's Eldfell cone and ideological divides in 1982 Berlin, Germany (right). Despite the increased coverage of controversial subjects, Society membership grew at a faster rate than ever before. By 1980 the Society had more than 10 million members.

Schaller trekked into the high mountains of South Asia to examine populations of wild sheep, goats, and the rare snow leopard. After weeks of stalking and watching, Schaller snapped the first photographs ever published of the "ghost cat of the Himalaya." Eugenie Clark, the "Shark Lady," was transforming our understanding of the ocean predators. Often disdaining steel "shark cages," she swam freely among these mysterious, fascinating creatures. At the same time, Roger Payne was studying humpback whales. A record of their haunting "songs" was bound into each copy of the January 1979 issue of *National Geographic*—and sparked the movement to ban whale hunting.

In Mexico's Sierra Madre, Catalina Aguado Trail (formerly Cathy Brugger) and husband Ken Brugger, volunteers with biologist Fred Urquhart's team, solved a long-standing mystery when they discovered the wintering grounds of the eastern North American monarch butterfly. Katharine Payne and Joyce Poole, working in Kenya and Namibia in the 1980s, revealed that elephants, who seemed to move as one toward water holes, communicate through infrasonic sounds, low-pitched rumblings carrying for miles across the landscape. Meanwhile, as Jane Goodall, Dian Fossey, and Biruté Galdikas continued demonstrating the close kinship between apes and humans, Francine (Penny) Patterson showed that an endangered lowland gorilla named Koko possessed marked linguistic skills. *Geographic* articles, books, and a Television Special, *Search for the Great Apes,* brought the stories of these important projects to the world.

These explorers had all been championed by Melvin M. Payne, Society President between 1967 and 1976, whose sharp eye for promising scientists matched his firm grip on business affairs. A strong proponent of field research, Payne himself spent

▲ **1975** With its debut, *World* magazine brought the stories and images of *National Geographic* to a younger audience. The magazine continues today as *National Geographic Kids.*

▼ **1977** "To Live in Harlem" was a milestone: the magazine's first article by Black journalists on Black life in the United States.

▲ **1985** Eugenie Clark struggles to untangle two sixgill sharks and a gummy shark caught on the same fishing longline.

▼ **1979** *Songs of the Humpback Whale* was inserted into the January 1979 *Geographic.*

▶ **1971** Trekking miles through remote Asia, biologist George Schaller shot the first images of the elusive snow leopard in the wild.

many months "under canvas" and was awarded the Conservation Service Medal, the Interior Department's highest honor, for his "leadership in exploration, research, and education."

In 1980 Gil Grosvenor gave up the editorship to become the Society's President. The creative and energetic Bill Garrett then became Editor of *National Geographic*. A magazine that had already grown to include subjects as disparate as rats and the Shroud of Turin now broadened even further. Articles ranged from the archaeology of garbage to the mystery of sleep to the sense of smell, complete with a scratch-and-sniff card to test readers' responses to key odors. Staff photographer James Stanfield negotiated the mazes of the Vatican and emerged with exclusive coverage.

Garrett also published a series of three-dimensional holographic covers, the first to appear on a mass-circulation magazine.

Above all, photojournalism flourished. Steve McCurry, a gutsy freelance photographer, brought back pictures of the contested Afghan frontier and the drought-stricken Sahel of Africa. Jodi Cobb gained entrée to the secluded world of Saudi women. Prizewinning writer Mike Edwards and photographer Steve Raymer covered the tragedy of the 1986 Chernobyl nuclear accident. And in 1981, in what would become the most popular article in *National Geographic* up to that point, Rowe Findley related the gripping story of the 1980 eruption of Mount St. Helens. "The shining Sunday morning turns forebodingly gray and to a blackness in which a hand cannot be seen in front of an eye. In the eerie gray and black, relieved only by jabs of lightning, filled with thunder and abrading winds, a thousand desperate acts of search and salvation are underway."

Meanwhile, explorers and adventurers pressed on in the old-fashioned way, one foot after another. In 1977 Peter and Barbara Jenkins completed a five-year walk across America. That same year, Robyn Davidson and four camels crossed 1,700 miles of Australian outback. Two years later and some 1,200 feet beneath the surface, Sylvia Earle strolled on the seafloor off Oahu wearing a pressurized hard-shell diving JIM suit. Twelve men had already visited the moon, but "Her Deepness" became the first human to walk untethered this deep in the sea. In 1986 polar explorer Will Steger completed the first successful unresupplied dogsled expedition to the North Pole since Peary's 1909 trip. And in 1980, armed with little more than ski poles and an ice ax, Reinhold Messner became the first

▲ **1975** A mystery solved: Volunteers from biologist Fred Urquhart's team, including Catalina Aguado Trail (above), discovered the wintering grounds of the eastern population of monarch butterflies.

▼ **1971** Named in honor of its discoverer, this rare orchid was found in Brazil by staff member Luis Marden.

PAGE BY PAGE

MAKING THE MAGAZINE

▸ **1998** Sporting 3D glasses, editorial staff attend a "wall walk," examining 3D photographs of Mars that were subsequently published in August.

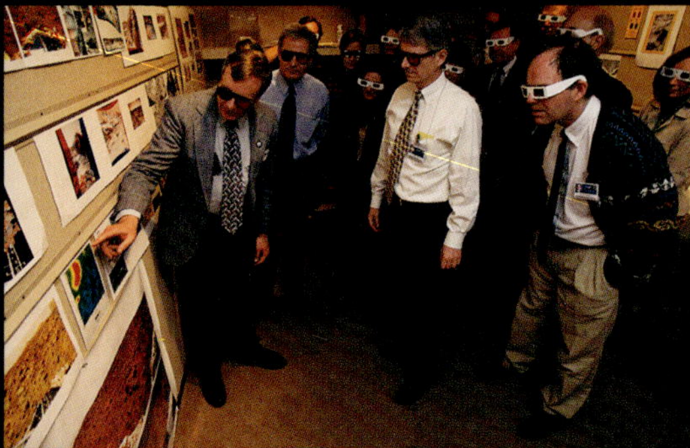

It starts as an idea, a story proposal on, let's pretend, Shangri-La, approved by the magazine's editors. A writer and a photographer are then assigned and dispatched to this mythical land.

Many weeks later, after fieldwork is done, photo editors comb through the resulting images, perhaps as many as 20,000, to find just the right ones, at most only several dozen, that best illustrate the story. Layout proceeds and text is polished. The article is rigorously checked for accuracy by research editors. The Editor in Chief always personally picks the cover picture. The finest paper and state-of-the-art presses then ensure the highest-quality printing. Finally, anywhere from several months to several years after it first began as an idea, members find in their mailboxes the *Geographic*'s latest on that place that is no place, Shangri-La. ■

▾ **1980s** Checked and rechecked and checked still again, a marked-up text proof vividly demonstrates the Research Division's scrupulous regard for accuracy.

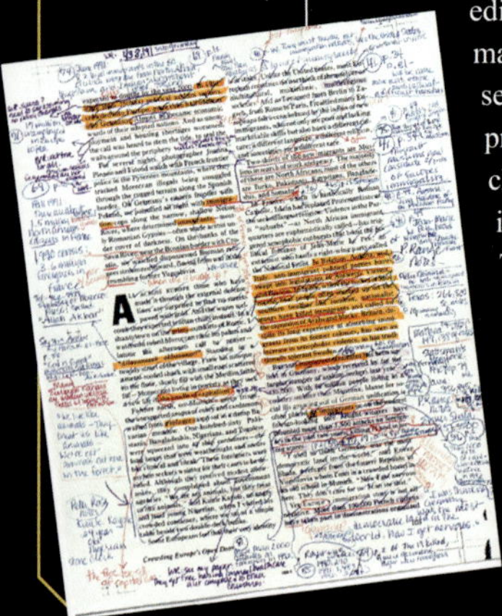

▲ **1985** Gaining unprecedented access to the Vatican, photographer Jim Stanfield gave readers a rare glimpse of Pope John Paul II alone in his garden, away from the crowds that followed his every movement.

person known to have summited Everest without bottled oxygen—and all alone. Messner wrote in the October 1981 *National Geographic,* "I want to experience the mountain as it really is ... By using an artificial oxygen supply, I feel I would no longer be climbing the mountain towering above me. I would simply be bringing its summit down to me."

Pluck and daring and originality of mind led Thor Heyerdahl, author of *Kon-Tiki,* to risk ocean voyages in boats made solely of papyrus reeds. Tim Severin imitated sixth-century Irish monk St. Brendan by sailing a leather boat from Ireland to Newfoundland, and followed in the imaginary wakes of Ulysses, Jason, and Sinbad across real seas. *National Geographic* Associate Editor Joseph

▸ **1985** Sharbat Gula, a young refugee from Soviet attacks in Afghanistan, didn't know for nearly two decades that her portrait had become the most famous cover image in the magazine's history.

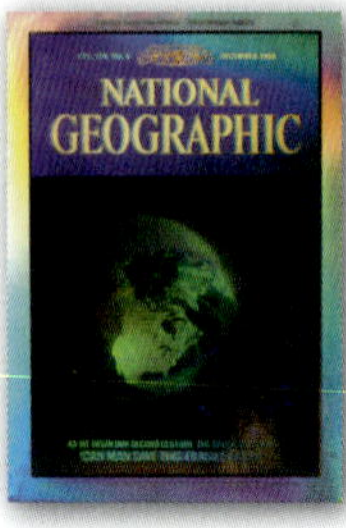

▲ **1988** Bruce Dale spent weeks photographing the shattering globe on the holographic cover for the December 1988 issue.

▶ **1981** Reinhold Messner made a solo ascent of Everest without oxygen, pausing for only 40 minutes at the summit.

▼ **1981** Coverage of the cataclysmic 1980 eruption of Mount St. Helens captured readers' attention like no other story in the magazine's history.

ST. HELENS
MOUNTAIN WITH A DEATH WISH

A gleaming white peak in the Cascades blasts away the top 1,300 feet of its crest in a massive eruption that takes dozens of lives, perils thousands of others, devastates 200 square miles, triggers destructive floods and mudflows, and sends ash clouds rolling across the Northwest. Twenty-one photographers capture the cataclysm in broad scope and stunning detail, and Assistant Editor Rowe Findley writes an intensely personal, three-part account of this first volcanic event in the contiguous 48 states in 63 years.

Judge and Luis Marden retraced the path of Christopher Columbus across the Atlantic, conjecturing that tiny Samana Cay in the Bahamas was the explorer's first landfall in the New World— not the nearby island of San Salvador, the generally accepted site.

Such voyages proved the capabilities of ancient—and not-so-ancient—mariners, readers of the magazine learned. As David Lewis related in December

▲ **1977** Covering communism, photographer Dean Conger captured this parade through Leningrad's Palace Square in celebration of the October 1917 revolution.

1974's "Wind, Wave, Star, and Bird," Polynesian navigators still found their way from one widely scattered island to the next by detecting the direction of swells and prevailing winds, monitoring submarine luminescence, and following the *kaveinga,* or "star path." Using the star path as his sole chart, Lewis sailed with his pilot, Tevake, 2,400 miles from the Society Islands to New Zealand. When he sighted his first headland 35 days later, he was only a few miles away from his intended target.

Exciting discoveries continued to be made. Marine geologist Robert Ballard explored the utter darkness of the deep sea in the Woods Hole Oceanographic Institution's submersible Alvin. In 1977 he joined a scientific expedition off the Galápagos Islands where, with the assistance of Alvin and *National Geographic* photographic expertise,

▼ **1977** Tom Canby and Jim Stanfield sampled a fried version of their subject for a 1977 story about the adaptable, resilient, and sometimes repulsive rat.

▲ **1985** Stopped for eternity, a pocket watch recovered shortly after *Titanic* sank records the moment of tragedy.

▸ **1991** Illuminated by the Russian *Mir I* submersible, the bow of the R.M.S. *Titanic* looms out of the deep.

the team found hydrothermal vents—hot water springs—in the seafloor. Clustered around the vents were giant clams and tube worms—the first life ever discovered dependent on Earth's fiery core for energy and not ultimately on the sun.

In 1985 Ballard made another amazing discovery. "I cannot believe my eyes," he wrote in the December 1985 *National Geographic*. "From the abyss two and a half miles beneath the sea the bow of a great vessel emerges in ghostly detail." It was the remains of *Titanic,* the most exciting shipwreck discovery of the time. Around the world, Bob Ballard became a household name and is now a National Geographic Explorer at Large.

▸ **1988** Perhaps the finest example of pre-Columbian jewelry ever found emerged from a secret chamber in the tomb of a Moche lord. The figurine at the center of this gold and turquoise ear ornament wears a headdress and an owl-heads necklace and has a war club. A skeleton found nearby wore similar attire.

Society-supported expeditions in East Africa continued to unearth tantalizing traces of our oldest ancestors. Richard Leakey discovered in Kenya a nearly complete skeleton of *Homo erectus,* our most immediate progenitor. Donald Johanson excavated in Ethiopia a treasure trove of *Australopithecus afarensis* fossils, perhaps three million years old, representing what may be one of the earliest branches on the human evolutionary tree. And Mary Leakey found fossilized hominin footprints in ancient Tanzanian volcanic ash that she dated at 3.6 million years old—evidence that human ancestors walked on two legs eons earlier than once thought.

▼ **1985** Entombed by the eruption that buried Pompeii in 79 C.E., this Roman woman's skeleton was discovered at nearby Herculaneum and was featured on the cover of *National Geographic* in July 1985. Among the woman's treasures were two golden rings, a pair of pierced earrings, and the solid gold snake-headed bracelets above.

While *National Geographic* published arresting photographs of the recently exhumed dead at Herculaneum, destroyed by the volcano Mount Vesuvius in 79 C.E., Kenan Erim and other archaeologists studied Aphrodisias, an astonishingly complete Greco-Roman city in Turkey. Grantee Christopher Donnan excavated untouched royal Inca tombs in Peru, and Norman Hammond explored Maya ones in Belize. One site, Hammond told readers, had all the makings of a childhood fantasy. "An ancient city lost under the green canopy of a remote jungle. Vines and roots snaking over temples and pyramids. And beneath it all, an undiscovered tomb containing the art of a vanished civilization and the skeletal remains of a long-dead nobleman."

New technologies—remote sensing, lasers, computer graphics, x-rays, and CT scans—allowed the Geographic to depict the world in new ways. One television documentary, *The Invisible World,* even

UNDER THE SEA

EXPLORING THE OCEAN REALM

▲ **1989** In the shadow of Japan's Mount Fuji, the robot Searover dips beneath the surface of Suruga Bay, which plunges to 26,250 feet. Explorers and photographers David Doubilet and Emory Kristof and marine biologist Eugenie Clark studied Suruga in 1989, recording the largest creature yet seen in the deep sea: a 23-foot sleeper shark.

"The best way to observe fish is to become a fish," said underwater pioneer Jacques-Yves Cousteau. Before Cousteau, large portions of Earth's vast oceans were largely unknown. National Geographic has devoted many grants and thousands of pages to the process of developing the technologies that allow us to become more like fish and to learn about the sea.

In 1960, shortly after Cousteau's accounts of underwater exploration with scuba equipment began appearing in the magazine, U.S. Navy Lt. Don Walsh and Jacques Piccard descended seven and a half miles in the bathyscaphe *Trieste* to the deepest spot in the ocean—the Mariana Trench. No one explored this area again for the next 52 years. But in March 2012, with National Geographic support, filmmaker James Cameron made the first solo dive to that same dark region.

The decades in between saw great advances in oceanography. In addition to Cousteau the Society supported Edwin Link, who led a series of experiments to test a human's ability to live and work in the deep ocean.

The topography of the ocean floor remained virtually unknown until Bruce Heezen and Marie Tharp completed a map of the ocean floor in the 1960s. The map revealed ridges and contours as rugged as any landscape on Earth, but much remained to be discovered. The Society participated in the deep-ocean experiments of Project FAMOUS, which made the first crewed descents to the Mid-Atlantic Ridge. A young oceanographer named Robert Ballard took part in this expedition and another in 1977 to the Galápagos Rift, where he and his colleagues discovered the first forms of life based not on photosynthesis but on chemosynthesis. Convinced that remotely operated vehicles could use sonar to view larger portions of the ocean floor, Ballard began developing the technologies that would lead to the discovery of *Titanic* in 1985. Since then, he has gone on to find numerous wrecks worldwide and traces of an ancient, cataclysmic flood in the Black Sea.

As quickly as they are being explored, the world's oceans are also being destroyed. Noted marine biologists Explorer at Large Sylvia Earle and Explorer in Residence Enric Sala have been persuading governments to preserve some of the world's remaining pristine ecosystems. The fight to protect our ocean realm continues. ■

▲ **1977** The discovery of life on deep-sea vents by Explorer Robert Ballard and his team was announced in the October 1977 *Geographic*.

◀ **1960s** The globe shows the topography of the ocean floor.

▼ **1979** Explorer Sylvia Earle descended to a record depth of 1,250 feet in this special JIM suit.

▲ **1984** Thousands of letters from Society members over the years inquired about travel to the destinations featured in *National Geographic* magazine. *National Geographic Traveler* launched in 1984. It is still published locally in nine countries around the world.

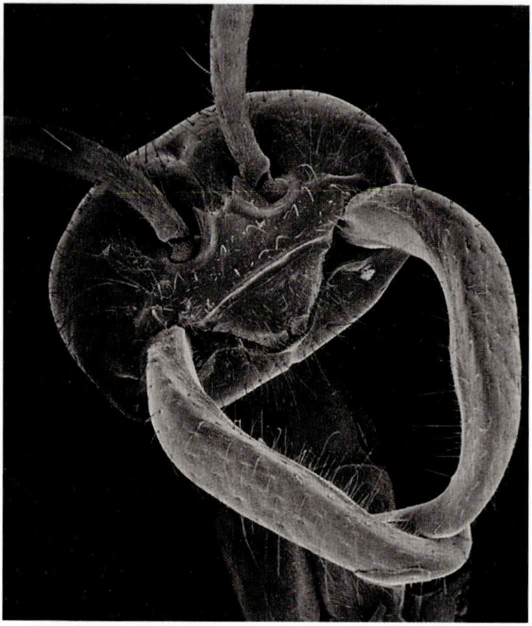

▶ **1974** This army ant is magnified 40 times its actual size under a scanning electron microscope.

▼ **1984** Art with a purpose: The beautiful diagrams and cutaways below visually explain the complicated structure of a strand of DNA.

showed an image, derived via electron microscope, of the dance of a single atom.

In fact, National Geographic was becoming as familiar for its magnificent television programs, appearing four times a year, as for its yellow-bordered magazine. Blockbusters like *The Incredible Machine* (1975), *The Sharks* (1982), and *Land of the Tiger* (1985) were among the most watched shows ever

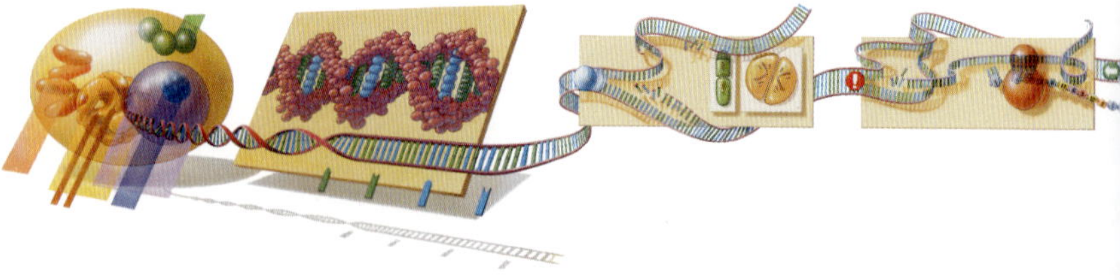

◂ **1970** A National Geographic film crew gets up close and personal for a Special about Ethiopia's crocodiles.

televised on PBS at that time. In 1985 *National Geographic Explorer* launched on cable television and featured episodes ranging from treks to Everest to venomous snakes to war in Afghanistan.

In 1984 the Geographic added a fourth building to its campus. Dedicating it, President Ronald Reagan observed that the Society over the years had "brought home the profound truth that we are … a human family living together on a tiny blue-and-green planet." Nevertheless, Gil Grosvenor was worried. "Pick up a newspaper and every single day

MAPPING THE WORLD

Since the first one was published in the magazine in 1888, maps have been an integral component of many magazine articles, books, and television programs produced by the Society. Originally drafted by hand on large projections, today's maps are created by cutting-edge software to chart everything from the Grand Canyon to the outer reaches of the universe.

▲ **1979** Testaments to eternity and to the fragility of our resources, the stone sentinels of Easter Island mark a land where resources may have been completely exploited, forcing the ancient islanders to leave. Will such a fate befall Earth? In 1988 National Geographic sponsored programs and seminars as part of its Earth '88 symposium to find solutions to the planet's problems.

you'll see how geography plays a dominant role in giving a third dimension on life," he wrote. But test results showed that American schoolchildren knew little geography.

Grosvenor set out to change that. He began a geography education program, harnessing a national network of teacher training programs funded by the specially created National Geographic Society Education Foundation. A National Geographic Bee for grades four through eight followed in 1989. And by 1994, a set of National Geography Standards would be drafted and adopted for use in the nation's classrooms.

In 1988 the National Geographic Society celebrated its centennial. Its facilities were now

◂ **1981** A world fast outstripping its resources became the focus of a special supplemental issue devoted to energy that was sent to all Society members.

◂ **1985** "You're nowhere unless you know where you are" became the mantra of Society President Gilbert M. Grosvenor, who undertook massive efforts to educate students about global relationships.

▴ **1981** Our precious planet seen from space

▾ **1988** Earth's "third pole," Mount Everest, was mapped in painstaking detail for the December 1988 issue of *National Geographic* magazine.

unrivaled, the reach of its publications and programs now global. It had supported more than 3,000 expeditions and research projects. Membership had passed 10 million. At a black-tie dinner President-elect George H.W. Bush presided over a celebration. Jacques-Yves Cousteau, Sir Edmund Hillary, Jane Goodall, Mary and Richard Leakey, and John Glenn were among the 15 Explorers who received special Centennial Awards for their contributions to exploration and discovery. The prize was a crystal globe, symbol of our fragile Earth. ■

BREITLING
ORBITER 3

THE HEART OF ADVENTURE

"Everyone is an explorer. How could you possibly live your life looking at a door and not go open it?"

ROBERT BALLARD

◂ **1999 Flying high over the Alps in the *Breitling Orbiter 3,* Bertrand Piccard and Brian Jones embark on the first nonstop circumnavigation of the globe by hot-air balloon. Almost 20 days and 29,018 miles later, on March 20, 1999, the two men achieved their goal.**

GORE-TEX

1989 Members of Will Steger's International Trans-Antarctica Expedition struggle through lunch.

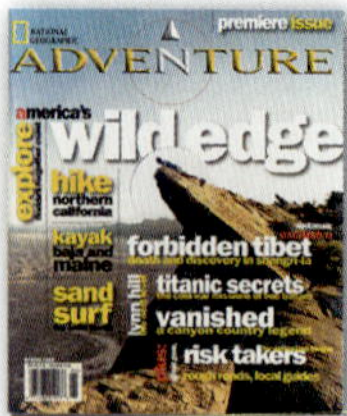

▲ **1999** For a decade following its 1999 debut, the award-winning *National Geographic Adventure* offered readers spine-tingling stories.

▶ **1990** Deep in the murky waters of Siberia's Lake Baikal, a joint Soviet-American team probes the abundant aquatic life of its unique ecosystem, which boasts more endemic species than any other lake. The expedition found that Baikal, the world's deepest lake, was once connected to the sea.

There is no better description of the spirit of modern adventure than that offered by Bertrand Piccard, who with Brian Jones in 1999 piloted *Breitling Orbiter 3* on the first nonstop hot-air balloon journey around the world. Writing in the September 1999 *National Geographic,* Piccard stated: "Human beings always want to control nature, but to fly around the world by balloon, even using our most advanced technology, we

◀ **1994** In April 1994 photographer William Albert Allard documented the heartbreak and the triumphs of "A Season in the Minors." Many of the photographs were later featured in a traveling exhibition.

must harmonize with nature, following the rhythm of the wind."

Harmonizing with nature has increasingly come to define the Geographic's approach to exploration. Acknowledging this shift, President Gilbert M. Grosvenor, during the 1988 centennial celebrations, asserted that the Society had begun its first century "with a determination to better understand the world," but that it should commence its second by also encouraging "a better stewardship of the planet."

▲ **1995** Going out on a limb—or on a line—*National Geographic* photographers go to great lengths to gain new angles on the world.

To highlight the reality that the planet was still imperfectly understood, the Society in 1995 instituted an Explorers in Residence program. Will Steger, veteran leader of treks to both poles, was first in a long line of very big names in exploration, each of whom would spend part of their time at headquarters and the remainder in the field. A glimpse of red feathers protruding from the ice led archaeologist Johan Reinhard, climbing high in the Peruvian Andes, to the mummy of a young Inca girl, dubbed the Ice Maiden. Study of her remains, more than 500 years old, has led to valuable insights regarding ancient Inca sacrificial burial. Two recreational spelunkers guided paleoanthropologist Lee Berger and his team to a monumental discovery in the Rising Star cave system 30 miles northwest of Johannesburg. In a chamber later named Dinaledi ("chamber of stars" in Sesotho, the region's common language), the cavers found remains scattered across the floor. Within two months, Berger's team had recovered more than 1,200 fossils from an area of roughly 10 square feet—the first of a new hominin species, *Homo naledi*.

▲ **1997** An expedition to Antarctica's remote Queen Maud Land is dwarfed by phantasmagoric peaks seldom seen by humans.

▲ **1969** Nzube Mutwiwa and Richard Leakey reassemble a fossil skull at Koobi Fora, Kenya.

Other Explorers in Residence have included Meave Leakey, director of the Koobi Fora camp on the shores of Kenya's Lake Turkana, where a number of important hominin fossils have been discovered. Her talented daughter, Louise, an Explorer at Large, works closely with her and represents the third generation of the Leakey family to work closely with the Geographic. Wade Davis, an ethnobotanist and student of Indigenous cultures, has lived among tribal peoples and is strongly committed to the preservation of their traditional ways.

Explorer at Large Bob Ballard not only has located the

wrecks of such World War II vessels as the *Bismarck, Yorktown,* and John F. Kennedy's *PT-109* but also has found evidence of a cataclysmic flood in the prehistoric Black Sea. And in March 2012 Hollywood director and Explorer at Large James Cameron made the first solo dive to the Pacific's Challenger Deep, the first person to visit that deepest spot in the ocean since balloonist Bertrand Piccard's father, Jacques, did in 1960, alongside Don Walsh.

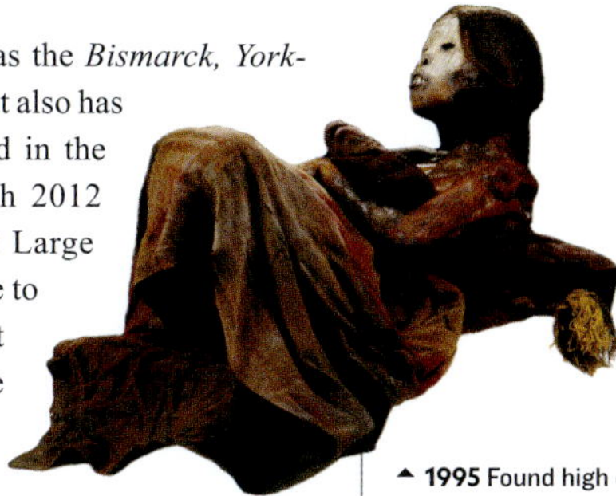

▲ **1995** Found high on an Andean peak, the "Ice Maiden" was sacrificed to the Inca gods about 500 years ago.

When President Gilbert M. Grosvenor retired in 1996 (and stepped down as Board Chairman in 2010), he left as his primary legacy a strong commitment to improving geography education at the primary and secondary school levels. Nevertheless, the family that had overseen the Society's growth and development since its founding now passed on the torch of leadership. Under John Fahey, Grosvenor's successor and the former head of Time-Life Books, a venturesome new Geographic emerged, one striving to "inspire people to care about the planet."

For instance, *National Geographic Traveler* magazine, published from 1984 to 2019, took the lead in promoting the sustainable travel practices known as geotourism. It even drew up a Geotourism Charter to protect the geographic character of travel destinations—harmonizing with nature again—that emphasizes conservation values and encourages local community

▲ **2002** Robert Ballard and his team study data during the search for John F. Kennedy's wrecked *PT-109* in the Solomon Islands. At left, a necklace ornament from a tomb in Abusir, near Cairo

▲ **1993** A special extra issue of *National Geographic* published in 1993 addressed the planet's water crisis.

▼ **2002** *National Geographic* increasingly tackled global health issues, including AIDS, overpopulation, and the war on disease.

involvement. Aspiring geotourists who desire to see for themselves something of Antarctica can always turn to National Geographic Expeditions. Guided by seasoned explorers and other experts, they can trek through Rwanda's Volcanoes National Park in search of mountain gorillas and golden monkeys, ascend the Andes by train to Machu Picchu, or voyage to remote Easter Island. Thanks to a partnership with Lindblad Expeditions, a pioneer in sustainable adventure travel, such geotourists can also cruise among the enchanted Galápagos Islands or along the edge of the polar ice packs.

Complementing such efforts to promote travel that harmonizes with the geographic character of places, the flagship *National Geographic* magazine reported on a variety of issues with global implications. Under Editors Bill Allen (1995–2004) and

OLD BONES

DIGGING FOR DINOSAURS

In 1907 *National Geographic* reported the discovery of "A Strange and Remarkable Beast"—a frozen mammoth recovered from the Siberian tundra. Since that moment paleontology—the study of life from past geologic periods—has captivated readers hungry for news of ancient beasts, especially dinosaurs. Roy Chapman Andrews thrilled readers with his discovery of the first intact nest of dinosaur eggs in Mongolia's harsh Gobi Desert. Andrews reported the find in *National Geographic,* peppering his account with tales of dodging bandits. Some say Andrews was the real-life inspiration for Indiana Jones.

Paleontology made tremendous leaps in the 20th century, and the Society has supported a number of top researchers in the field, including Thomas Rich and Patricia Vickers-Rich, who shed light on "the dinosaurs of darkness," polar dinosaurs who inhabited Australia when it was still attached to Antarctica. Society grantees discovered the fossil of the world's largest lemur in Madagascar and the remains of the world's oldest grasses in present-day Nebraska and Kansas. Phil Manning discovered an exceptionally well-preserved dinosaur mummy in North Dakota. With soft tissue encased in an envelope of skin, the mummy helped unlock secrets about the evolution of dinosaurs.

▲ **1925** Roy Chapman Andrews cradles a fossil dinosaur egg discovered in the Gobi Desert.

◀ **1998** Skull of *Tyrannosaurus rex*

▼ **1990s** Workers uncover a prehistoric rhinoceros in present-day Nebraska.

Chris Johns (2005–2014; he took home 21 National Magazine Awards during his time at the helm), the *Geographic* published stories on worldwide pandemics, the inhumane side of the diamond trade, and weapons of mass destruction alongside those announcing new archaeological discoveries or profiling scientific wonders. Articles on Somalia, malaria, nuclear waste, and Afghan women were honored with prestigious accolades like the Overseas Press Club Award, while praise was heaped on single-topic issues concerning Africa or the growing scarcity of water resources. And as the magazine transitioned to the digital era, subscribers to its mobile version enjoyed such unique treats as a slow-motion video of a sprinting cheetah shot with a Phantom high-definition digital camera.

Furthermore, the yellow-bordered journal began crossing other borders with dispatch. In 1995, when the Geographic launched a Japanese-language edition, the magazine went truly

▾ **1995** *National Geographic* began publishing local-language editions across the globe.

▸ **2004** Tearing across the prairie, a tornado sweeps up viewers on the increasingly popular National Geographic Channel.

international. At their height, 36 local-language editions—including Chinese, Korean, Arabic, Hebrew, and Bahasa Indonesian as well as those in nearly every tongue spoken from Spain to the Urals—were being printed each month. The impact was astonishing: One in four members read *National Geographic* in a language other than English.

▲ **2012** Photographer Frans Lanting captured a herd of zebra racing through Kenya's Masai Mara National Reserve.

The success of the National Geographic Channel has had an even greater international impact. The National Geographic Channel debuted in 1997, initially in Europe, Asia, and Australia, and soon became the fastest-growing channel in the world. Two years after the January 2001 premiere of the domestic counterpart, it too was reaching more than 40 million homes. A decade later those numbers had skyrocketed. While the Society's Television Specials and Explorer programs amassed even more

▸ **2000** "Are we alone?" asked an article in the January 2000 issue, which heralded the new millennium and introduced a design first: the futuristic alteration of the cover type.

▲ **1998** In the control room of his research vessel, Robert Ballard, discoverer of *Titanic, PT-109,* and other famous shipwrecks, carefully watches a video monitor. A National Geographic Explorer at Large, Ballard pioneered deep-sea exploration via remotely operated vehicles.

▸ **2005** *March of the Penguins,* a National Geographic co-production, won the 2005 Academy Award for Best Documentary Feature.

Emmys (well over 100), the National Geographic Channels—for there were a multitude of them, including Nat Geo Wild, Nat Geo Adventure, and the Spanish-language network Nat Geo Mundo in addition to the original Channel—were the engines driving the Society's international growth, being beamed in 37 languages to some 435 million households in 173 countries.

Nevertheless, the Society didn't confine itself to the small screen. It also produced feature films. In November 2000, while making *Frontline Diaries: Into the Forbidden Zone,* writer Sebastian Junger was among the last Western journalists to interview legendary Afghan resistance leader Ahmad Shah Massoud. A decade later Junger was back in the Hindu Kush, embedded with a U.S. Army airborne unit engaged in combat operations against Taliban forces in a remote valley dubbed the "deadliest place on Earth." *Restrepo,* the Geographic-produced film he directed during this deployment, was nominated for a 2010 Academy Award.

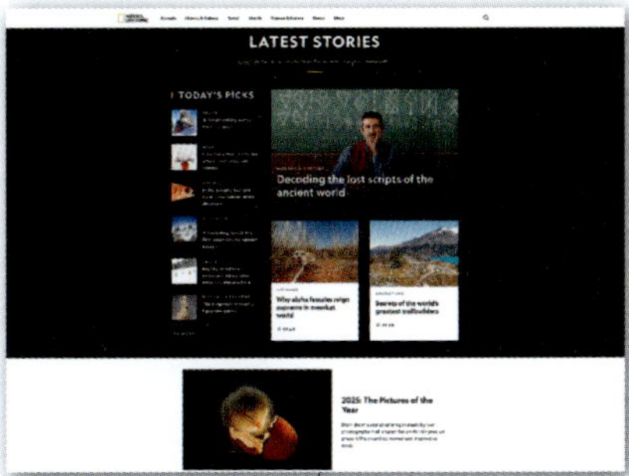

▲ **2026** Continuing National Geographic's tradition of embracing new technology, the Society launched its website in 1996 (shown here in its 2026 iteration) with offerings of news, blogs, stories, maps, photographs, and a wealth of other resources.

Five years earlier the Society's *March of the Penguins* had actually won the coveted Oscar, honored for being that year's best documentary feature. The epic tale of the emperor penguins' urge to merge and the tribulations the birds were willing to undertake in order to raise chicks in the harshest place on Earth attracted long lines of moviegoers to cinemas all over the world. Twenty years later, *Secrets of the Penguins* revealed even more behaviors of the 18 species of penguins scattered across the globe. And in 2019 a very different but no less moving saga, *Free Solo,* won an Oscar. An account of Alex Honnold's ropeless climb up the face of Yosemite's El Capitan, the

◀ **1997** Inventor Mark W. Tilden shows off a few of his robotic creations: tiny insect robots that are powered by the sun. *National Geographic* caught up with the "Robot Revolution" in the July 1997 issue.

▸ **2024** Explorer at Large Nalini Nadkarni studies the unique ecosystems found in treetops. Here, she climbed to her preferred perch via a "master caster," a rope-throwing gadget of her own devising.

SMILE, YOU'RE ON CRITTERCAM

What would it be like to swim alongside a shark? The question inspired a prototype for the now famous National Geographic Crittercam, a special lightweight video camera (seen below strapped to an American alligator) that has given scientists new glimpses into behavior never before observed in sharks, marine mammals, and even lions—and presented viewers with an animal's-eye view of the world.

documentary was made by Explorers Elizabeth Chai Vasarhelyi and Jimmy Chin, who is a noted climber himself.

The Society sought out even larger screens. Its *Mysteries of Egypt* and *Lewis and Clark* broke records at large-format IMAX theaters. *Forces of Nature* and *Roar: Lions of the Kalahari* loomed gigantically out of the dark. And there had never been a concert picture quite as spectacular as 2008's *U2 3D,* which was quite popular with viewers (wearing polarized glasses) in several countries. The Society was proud to distribute it, not only because it was the first live-action, digital 3D film ever made but also because U2 was a band with

▲ **1996** After crossing 775 rugged miles of the Alaska Range, cyclists descend a thousand feet into Black Rapids Glacier.

planetary appeal that also possessed a planetary perspective. It was a "band of the world" and, according to John Fahey, "world music is something the Geographic as an institution is really interested in."

It was interested in a number of other subjects, too, as even a cursory glance at the Society's website revealed. Nat Geo Music could indeed be found there, as could breaking news stories on new scientific discoveries; blogs contributed by far-flung correspondents and photographers; information on environmental issues; a *Green Guide* promoting more

◂ **2008** National Geographic's *Green Guide*, available at the time on *nationalgeographic.com*, featured eco-friendly consumer choices.

THE WAITING GAME

NATURE PHOTOGRAPHY: A STANDARD OF EXCELLENCE

"Wandering off into nature is not geography," grumbled one critical board member after a series of startling photographs made by pioneer wildlife photographer George Shiras 3rd were published in the July 1906 *National Geographic*. To most people today, however, wandering off into nature is what National Geographic does best.

Even before improved films, faster cameras, and telephoto lenses allowed more striking results, National Geographic photographers have been willing to wait patiently in blinds for hours upon hours, prey to flies and mosquitoes, sun and heat, rain and cold—to undergo almost any tribulation—to

▼ **2019** An arctic wolf inspects the ATV that photographer Ronan Donovan and his team used to track wolves on Ellesmere Island in the Canadian Arctic.

◂ **1998** Light filters through a towering grove of giant kelp in the rich waters off California's Channel Islands. Photographer David Doubilet has circled the globe capturing the glory of vanishing coral reefs and the astonishing beauty and variety of the world's oceans. Doubilet, whose work has appeared in the magazine for five decades, is a National Geographic Explorer.

get just the right picture of birds on the wing or animals on the move.

As a result, every kind of nature photography has found expression somewhere at the Geographic, whether in the pages of the magazines or books or in the television documentaries that have won more than 30 Emmys and every major award for wildlife films. Whether it's the changing world of an apple tree or curious pictures of bizarre insects and strange wildflowers or the immemorial drama of predator and prey on the shimmering African plains, whether it is the stunning glory of reef and fish or the graceful arc of a breaching whale or the dangerous proximity of the shark, nature photography has come to play a fundamental role in the Geographic's presentation of the world. ■

▾ **1982** Captured in midair, an armadillo leaps in a fright reflex. "The Astonishing Armadillo" was featured in June.

◂ **1997** Patience and technical resourcefulness are essential for success

▸ **2003** Deep in the heart of Central Africa, elephants ford a stream in the Republic of the Congo's Nouabalé-Ndoki National Park.

sustainable living (while also explaining how the Geographic's own headquarters recycled trash and conserved energy); teaching resources; weird and wacky facts; cool clicks for kids; and of course maps, photos, video clips, and a ubiquitous button: Learn More. Upwards of 20 million people a month visited this online bazaar of information. When combined with the Society's television efforts, feature films, *National Geographic* circulation, the durably popular *National Geographic Kids* and *National Geographic Little Kids* magazines, and an array of exhibitions and live events, that number swelled 20-fold: The Society reached hundreds of millions of people a month, around the clock as around the globe. No wonder Fahey once commented, "National Geographic is an incredible mix of science and education, of

▸ **1999** Biologist and conservationist Mike Fay made a 15-month trek across some of Africa's most inhospitable terrain. Traveling lightly, with little more than a backpack and this wrist compass (below), Fay observed and recorded information about unspoiled wilderness and animals that had no fear of humans.

media and mission, of storytellers and explorers, all working to inspire people to care about the planet."

It can be grueling work, though. On September 20, 1999, Explorer Michael Fay stepped off into the bush of the Republic of the Congo. For the next 15 months the wildlife biologist crossed more than 2,000 miles of pristine Central African rainforest—on foot, wearing sandals, following a line straight through seemingly impenetrable forest. Battling leeches, scorpions, parasites, and driving rain, plunging through swamps, dodging vipers and deadly Ebola virus, encountering animals that had seen few, if any, human beings, Fay amassed an unprecedented amount of information about a

▲ **1989** A lone baobab tree in the Australian outback

▸ **2012** Krithi Karanth (at left)—the National Geographic Society's 10,000th research grantee—assesses human-wildlife conflicts in India's Western Ghats.

▴ **1989** National Geographic launched the yearly National Geographic Bee, a contest that awarded scholarships to its finalists. Now the Society hosts the Slingshot Challenge, focused on youth-led solutions for protecting our planet and improving our future.

still remarkably unspoiled wilderness. Through digital installments and three *National Geographic* articles, Fay's Megatransect transfixed the imagination of millions. Staff photographer Michael "Nick" Nichols's spellbinding photographs captured the primordial enchantment of this "green abyss" and helped persuade the government of Gabon to set aside 10 percent of its national territory—forests that might otherwise have gone to timber companies—to create 13 national parks.

Meanwhile, Fay's fellow Explorers have been matching his achievements by helping preserve those "rainforests of the sea," coral reefs. In 2006, for instance, Sylvia Earle helped persuade President George W. Bush to establish what is now called the Papahānaumokuākea Marine National Monument, nearly 140,000 square miles of ocean, coral, and island stretching northwest of Oahu and Hawaii—a reserve larger than all the U.S. national parks (outside Alaska) combined. It provides rookeries for 14 million seabirds, as well as refuges for both the endangered Hawaiian monk seal and the threatened green sea turtle. Papahānaumokuākea also contains the nation's most extensive coral reefs, home to some 7,000 marine species, half of which can be found nowhere else.

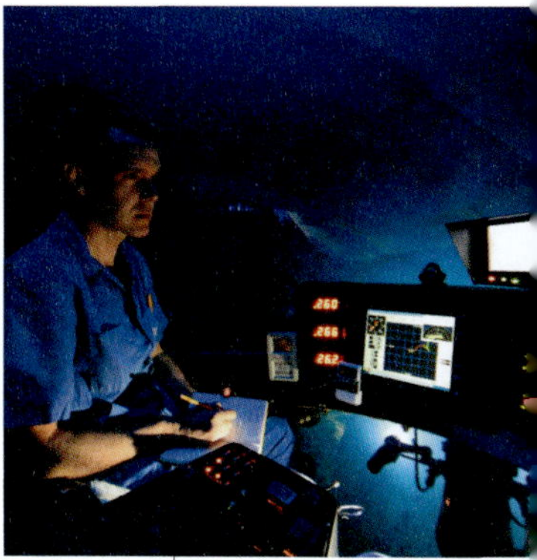

▲ **2013** Off the coast of Chile's San Felix Island, Explorer in Residence Enric Sala documents observations of deep-sea fauna from the DeepSee submersible.

Soon afterward, Enric Sala—who, while growing up in Spain, had been inspired to become a marine ecologist by watching Jacques-Yves Cousteau on television—launched the Society's Pristine Seas initiative, an effort to illuminate and protect our oceans' resilient ecosystems. His efforts have resulted in Chile establishing a 58,000-square-mile marine park around the island of Salas y Gómez, and Costa Rica creating a reserve almost as large around Cocos Island. Since 2008, Pristine Seas has helped establish 30 of

◀ **2007** Marine predators, like these gray reef sharks and red snappers hovering over the Pacific Ocean's Kingman Reef, indicate healthy coral reef ecosystems.

▲ **2011** Gerlinde Kaltenbrunner is the first woman to summit all 14 of the world's 8,000-meter peaks without using supplementary oxygen.

the largest marine protected areas in the world, covering a total area of 2.7 million square miles—more than twice the size of India.

Such achievements echo that "better stewardship of the planet" to which the Society was pledged. Indeed, John Fahey reiterated that "conservation is a key component of our mission in the 21st century." It's clear, then, that in the coming years many of the explorers who will be associated with National Geographic will be concerned with ecological issues such as dwindling resources, overpopulation, and the looming extinction of cultural and biological diversity.

When in 2011 Krithi Karanth received Society funding to examine human-wildlife interactions in India, it was the 10,000th research grant the Geographic had awarded in the century and a quarter of its existence. Daughter of one of the Indian subcontinent's most prominent wildlife biologists, Karanth represents a new generation of explorers that, in her words, feels the responsibility to "act now using the best science and link it to constructive, on-ground conservation action."

Digital expeditions represent another avenue for inquiry. Albert Lin, for example, hoped to solve a long-standing mystery—the whereabouts of Genghis Khan's tomb—without turning a spadeful of dirt. He perused satellite imagery of Mongolia and turned to the internet for help. Hundreds

DIGITAL EXPLOSION

With one click, the world of National Geographic is literally at hand. With the launch of *nationalgeographic.com* in the summer of 1996, exploration became interactive. Social media brought even more opportunities for connection—and photo sharing, too. By 2025 there were more than 270 million followers on Instagram, 50 million on Facebook, and more than 25 million on YouTube. The flagship website now logs more than 10 million visitors a month.

of volunteers analyzed thousands of images, geotagging landscape features that might be promising clues. Seeking to mount similar geotagging of satellite imagery to better estimate the number of refugees fleeing violence in Somalia, the United Nations Refugee Agency approached Explorer Patrick Meier. "Digital expeditions like these can democratize the next frontier of exploration," Meier says.

▼ **2012** James Cameron's Deepsea Challenger undergoes a test-dive.

Whether it be people geotagging satellite images of Mongolia from their living room or joining forces with wildlife filmmakers Dereck and Beverly Joubert—who, alarmed at the precipitous fall in the numbers of lions, tigers, leopards, snow leopards, and jaguars, established the Society's Big Cats Initiative, urging people everywhere to "cause an uproar"—there is a growing consensus, faced with the challenges we confront today, that we can accomplish more together than we can individually.

Hence, as the Society entered the 2010s, it refocused its attention on worldwide issues, endangered ecosystems, and of course adventure—but always adventure with a larger purpose. Filmmaker Sandesh Kadur, for instance, a National Geographic Explorer since 2013, became famous not only for working in remote locations but also for spotting behaviors and species new to science. His first documentary, *Sahyadris: Mountains of the Monsoon,* showcased the richness of

▼ **2011** A film clip of a honey badger eating anything it encounters, including a viper, went viral when a comic version was uploaded to YouTube.

▲ **2013** Photographer Beverly Joubert used the roots of a baobab tree as a frame for this image of herself and Dereck Joubert.

▶ **2009** A colossal face coalesces from a pillar of gas and dust in the Carina Nebula.

India's Western Ghats and helped the vulnerable region win recognition as a UNESCO World Heritage site in 2012.

Kirsten Elstner was a successful freelance photographer for the *New York Times* and other publications when the tragedies of September 11 inspired her to do something more to foster a sense of global kinship. In 2003 she partnered with the Society, and National Geographic Photo Camp was born. Year after year, Photo Camp brings together young people in locations around the

◀ **2008** A special issue devoted entirely to one country, the May 2008 *National Geographic* explores the "terrain of exuberance and anxiety that is China today."

world for a multiday workshop with National Geographic photographers, Explorers, teachers, and community members. There they learn not only camera skills but also how to build confidence and listen to each other and to their peers.

As always, the Society's ventures ranged from the stars to the depths, but more than ever they included participants from every part of the world, unafraid to tackle some of the globe's most pressing problems. ■

▲ **1995** Chris Johns gets a bird's-eye view of East Africa's Rift Valley.

◀ **2012** National Geographic Kids launched this book series full of "tantalizing tidbits" for readers ages seven to 10.

CHAPTER 6

2014-PRESENT

A COMMUNITY OF EXPLORERS

"We are showing people that history isn't just something that you read in a textbook."

JUSTIN DUNNAVANT

◀ 2024 Cave divers prepare to enter Devil's Ear, a limestone rift at the bottom of Florida's Santa Fe River that gushes with crystal clear groundwater from an underlying aquifer. Devil's Ear is one of Florida's 33 first-magnitude springs, which discharge at least 64 million gallons of water a day.

2021 Water percolating into freezing alpine caves like this one, high in the Tennen Mountains south of Salzburg, Austria, sculpts itself into huge icicles, cones rising from below, and floor-covering cascades.

▲ **2017** With California's Yosemite Valley far beneath him, Alex Honnold free solos—a type of climbing that doesn't employ ropes or safety gear—up a crack on the 3,000-foot southwest face of El Capitan.

As the 21st century entered its adolescence, the planet faced new challenges from climate change, habitat loss, and political upheaval. National Geographic evolved accordingly. Though still delighted with individual tales of adventure—see the 2018 Oscar-winning documentary *Free Solo* for some nail-biting thrills—the organization realized that today's global issues needed global teams tackling them: a worldwide community of Explorers. Geographic's strengths in science, exploration, education, and storytelling could be leveraged by working hand in hand with regional leaders, educators, scientists, inventors, writers, photographers, and others. From the ground up, these groups could bring local knowledge

◂ **2019** Honnold's feat became a cover story for the magazine after being the subject of a 2018 Oscar-winning documentary for National Geographic Documentary Films.

and specialized skills to the quest to protect wildlife, safeguard ecosystems, look into the past, and communicate with the wider world.

In 2015 the Society partnered with 21st Century Fox to form a media company—National Geographic Partners. Disney's purchase of 21st Century Fox in 2019 resulted in the Society and Disney teaming up to amplify the Society's mission, bringing bold and distinctive storytelling to billions around the world. This landmark moment was overseen by Society CEO Gary Knell, who then became the CEO of National Geographic Partners. Tracy Wolstencroft took the helm as CEO of the National Geographic Society. In 2020 Dr. Jill Tiefenthaler became the first woman to hold the position of Society CEO, and she reinforced the mission to illuminate and protect the wonder of our world. The opening of National Geographic's revamped headquarters (known as Base Camp) in 2026, complete with a dynamic new Museum of Exploration, means the stories around this vital mission are inspiring more people than ever.

▲ **2026** The Museum of Exploration (shown here as a rendering) opens in National Geographic's revamped headquarters in Washington, D.C., with immersive exhibitions, theater, and outdoor displays.

◀ **2026** In this rendering of the courtyard of the updated campus, each planter represents a global ecosystem.

▸ **2024** Paleontologist and Explorer Diego Pol examines dinosaur remains belonging to titanosaur sauropods found in Argentina.

▾ **2023** A life-size replica of the sauropod *Patagotitan,* one of the largest land animals ever found, towers over the Patagonian city of Trelew.

With reinvigorated focus areas on wildlife, ocean, land, human histories and cultures, planetary health, and space, a new generation of Explorers has stepped into the picture. Hailing from Argentina to Afghanistan, they are as bold and adventurous as their legendary National Geographic forebears, and they're out to tackle big problems by employing large doses of ingenuity, teamwork, and communication skills. Like their 20th-century counterparts, they climb mountains, plunge into oceans, and trek through jungles. They also teach schoolchildren, collaborate with local leaders, invent high-tech tools, and spread knowledge online.

And they still make discoveries. Paleontologist Diego Pol has made one impressive find after another. Some of the most spectacular have come from Patagonia, where the Explorer and his colleagues from Argentina's Egidio Feruglio paleontology museum have unearthed fossils from some of the largest creatures ever to walk the earth, including bones from at least six specimens of a sauropod they named *Patagotitan*. The long-necked herbivore spanned an estimated 120 feet from head to tail and weighed some 70 tons. (That makes it as long as two subway cars end to end and heavier than 10 African elephants.)

▾ **2024** A skull model of *Koleken inakayali,* a recently discovered carnivorous dinosaur

Elsewhere in Argentina, the team discovered another sauropod, but this one was relatively small. *Titanomachya gimenezi* would have been about 20 feet long and weighed between five and 10 tons—about the size of a cow, if a cow had a weirdly long neck and tail. The size extremes embodied by these creatures may be tied, suggest Pol and

▲ **2011** Five and a half tons of smuggled ivory are lit aflame by the government of Kenya. Ivory stockpiles are frequently destroyed to take the contraband off the market and send a message to poachers.

his colleagues, to the changing environments of the late Cretaceous, when oceans began to encroach on the warm, humid terrain in South America.

Some Explorers have doubled as investigators into wildlife smuggling, a role that can come with considerable danger attached. "For too long in too many countries (including the U.S.), placing the word 'wildlife' in front of the word 'crime' had diminished its seriousness," wrote journalist Bryan Christy in his 2010 *National Geographic* article, "The Kingpin." Christy, an Explorer since 2014, conducted daring investigations into the illegal ivory trade, a lucrative business that has slaughtered hundreds of thousands of elephants for their tusks. His stories, as well as National Geographic's related documentaries, *Battle for the Elephants* and *Warlords of Ivory,* helped persuade China to shut down its domestic ivory market in 2017.

▸ **2015** "To protect wildlife and stop criminals, people first have to know the stories," says Bryan Christy. For the September 2015 issue, he teamed up with photographer Brent Stirton to illuminate those affected by the illegal ivory trade.

▲ **2023** Writer Sharon Guynup captures photographer Steve Winter in action with a selfie. The two won the 2024 Eliza Scidmore Award for their reporting on captive tigers in the United States.

The work of photographer Steve Winter and writer Sharon Guynup also led to policy change, this time in the United States. A longtime nature photographer, Winter turned his attention away from big cats in the wild to those in captivity. He and Guynup tracked down tiger breeders and the roadside zoos and county fairs where big cats were exhibited for paying audiences. The resulting *National Geographic* article spurred a national law protecting captive cats in 2022.

In India's Western Ghats, the tigers' home territories, another Explorer was taking an equally fruitful approach toward protecting big cats and their wild neighbors. It began at the 2017 National Geographic Explorers Festival in Washington, D.C., where biologist Krithi Karanth and photographer Gabby Salazar fell into conversation. "We just got talking," Karanth says, "and I told her, 'One of the things I'd really like to do is figure out a conservation program created for Indian children that uses education, art, storytelling, and games to inspire children who live around wildlife in India.'"

▼ **2013** A hidden camera catches Hollywood's most reclusive star: this male cougar known as P-22. A radio collar tracked his moves, but residents rarely glimpsed him.

Within a year, the two Explorers had started a program they named Wild Shaale (*shaale* means "school" in the Kannada language of India's Karnataka state). The program trains educators to teach children in village schools about local wildlife, helping them understand how animal and human needs overlap and building a sense of empathy and connection to the life around them.

▲ **2024** Krithi Karanth distributes illustrated storybooks designed by the Centre for Wildlife Studies to students in Karnataka, India.

Like Karanth, Dr. David Gruber, a marine biologist, also had something he wanted to do, and he found the way to do it by connecting with another Explorer. Would it be possible, he wondered, to translate the complex, clicking vocalizations of sperm whales into something humans could understand? Perhaps scientists could use machine learning—a branch of artificial intelligence—to decipher whale language, which he compares to digital data transfer.

Gruber reached out to Dr. Shane Gero, principal investigator of the Dominica Sperm Whale Project, who had been recording the animals' vocalizations. Their collaboration, dubbed Project CETI, employs a team of interdisciplinary experts to take on the huge task of recording whale calls, observing the corresponding

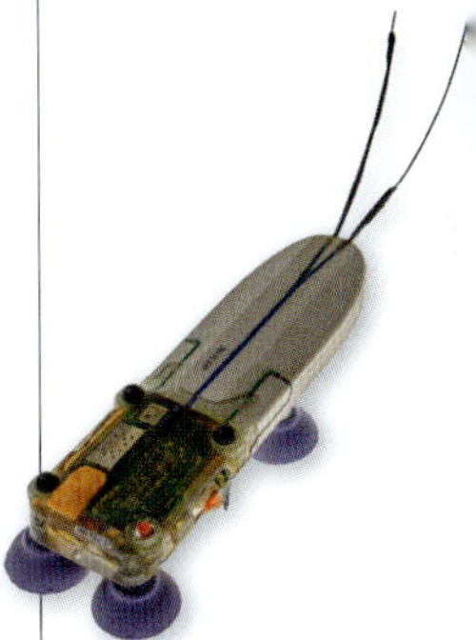

▲ **2024** This acoustic whale tag is equipped with silicone suction cups.

◀ **2024** In Dominica, Project CETI uses drones to tag whales and collect audio of their speech, which is then cataloged by AI.

LIVES OF THE PENGUINS

PROTECTING FLIGHTLESS BIRDS

▸ **2025** Pablo García Borboroglu is inspired by penguins' resilience: "When you see penguins making that big effort, you say, 'How can I give up?'"

▾ **2025** As members of the Global Penguin Society, Borboroglu and Candela Tisera Manochio study and protect the world's 18 penguin species and the lands and oceans they inhabit.

Pablo "Popi" García Borboroglu personally thanks the penguins he works with. "Every time we measure them or deploy a track," says the marine biologist, "I like to thank them because they're making a contribution: 'Thank you for carrying this. Thank you for bringing the information.'"

García Borboroglu, the president and chief scientific officer of the Global Penguin Society, has followed a career path that blends penguin research, conservation, and habitat protection. With his colleagues, he has been outfitting the birds with trackers—and in some cases, National Geographic Crittercams—to watch underwater penguin life firsthand. As they follow diverse penguin species around the world, from New Zealand to Antarctica, the researchers learn how penguins breed, grow, and travel. The biologist's organization has protected some 32 million acres of marine and coastal habitat to date; in 2025, García Borboroglu and his colleague, filmmaker and Explorer Bertie Gregory, were named the Rolex National Geographic Explorers of the Year. ■

whale behavior, and feeding vast amounts of data into computers. Early results are encouraging, as the researchers are already identifying significant musical patterns in the big mammals' communications.

Gruber and Gero's high-tech approach highlights an underlying driver of Explorer work: ingenuity. Explorers and their teams frequently need to be inventors as well, and their inventions are often dedicated to seeing the unseen, to venturing where human sight cannot penetrate. Explorer Ved Chirayath, an expert on aerial sensing devices, has applied technology originally designed for searching the night sky to imaging the ocean floor. Legendary oceanographer and Explorer at Large Sylvia Earle set him on this path: "She pulled me aside in the way that she does," he recalls, "and she said, 'You can take all of your talents and devote them to space. You can also devote them to protecting Earth, and here's why you should do it.'" Since that fateful conversation, he has invented drone-based sensing systems that can penetrate waves and murky waters to survey the land below. The resulting scans map previously unseen terrain and help scientists track the effects of climate change on delicate subsea ecosystems.

Cynthia Chiang, an Explorer since 2022, also uses

▲ **2021** Sperm whales, including this adult and calf swimming near the Caribbean nation of Dominica, communicate in clicks.

▼ **2022** Explorer Ved Chirayath invented an instrument called MiDAR (Multispectral Imaging, Detection, and Active Reflectance), which can scan the ocean floor to great depths using blue and ultraviolet laser light.

▲ **2024** Explorer and cosmologist Cynthia Chiang and her team set up two **ALBATROS** antennas at Uapishka Station in northern Québec to pick up radio wavelengths from the early universe.

advanced instruments to detect what has been hidden from human eyes—although she is peering at the farthest reaches of outer space. As a cosmologist, her goal is to learn more about the very early universe, from the "dark ages" before stars took shape to the moments of their fiery birth.

Radiation from this era, more than 13 billion years ago, reaches Earth only as faint radio waves, and in most spots on Earth it is lost inside a competing torrent of transmissions. To evade this radio competition, Chiang and her team are setting up an array of radio telescopes in some of the most remote regions of the world: subantarctic Marion Island in the Indian Ocean and Axel Heiberg Island in Canada's Arctic Ocean. The new assembly on Axel Heiberg, called ALBATROS (Array of Long Baseline Antennas for Taking Radio Observations from the Sub-Antarctic/Seventy-ninth parallel), will consist of eight radio telescopes working together to pick up murmurs from the ancient cosmos.

Some exploration relies on cameras and high-speed transmissions, and some requires learning to slow down and listen—particularly when it comes to understanding the interactions among people, landscapes, and history. Perhaps the most extreme example of the latter is National Geographic Explorer and

◂ **2013** In his trademark cowboy hat, Paul Salopek trudges across Ethiopia's Afar region and onto the December 2013 cover. With him are Suma'atuli (Branded on the Ear), the larger of the two camels, and A'urta (Traded for a Cow).

◂ **2018** Explorer Paul Salopek rows along the Ganges in Varanasi, Hinduism's holiest city. Although the murky water carries the ashes of some 30,000 people whose bodies are cremated there each year, the faithful believe it is pure enough to drink.

Pulitzer Prize–winning journalist Paul Salopek's Out of Eden Walk, which began in January 2013 and is still in progress.

Salopek is retracing humanity's ancient migration out of Africa by walking 23,612 miles from Ethiopia to the southernmost tip of South America—occasionally boarding a boat to cross bodies of water (the Black Sea, the Yellow Sea, the Pacific Ocean) that block his way. He calls his work "slow journalism." Every 100 miles, Salopek stops to log a milestone in the journey by photographing his surroundings and asking the nearest person the same three questions: Who are you? Where do you come from? Where are you going? Walking, oftentimes with local partners, through history at three miles an hour, he is connecting past and present.

Also on foot (often) are the citizen storytellers of 2892 Miles to Go, named for the length of the contiguous United States. This collaborative project, led by Explorer Ashley Lamb-Sinclair, connects young people with community leaders and educators to collectively solve real-life problems in their communities. Young people dive deep into local issues, exploring the past and current state of the community in order to create well-researched, compelling solutions for the future using geospatial data and mapping tools like ArcGIS StoryMaps.

▾ **2024** As part of National Geographic Photo Camp and the 2892 Miles to Go program, students document the natural world through both artwork and photographs.

FROM THE HEIGHTS TO THE DEPTHS

PERPETUAL PLANET EXPEDITIONS CHART EARTH'S KEY ENVIRONMENTS

The National Geographic Society entered its fourteenth decade determined to think big. The National Geographic and Rolex Perpetual Planet Expeditions—globe-spanning research into the planet's vital mountains, rainforests, and oceans—are one of its most ambitious ventures. An expansion of the Society's seven-decade partnership with Rolex, this multiyear, multicontinent, multidisciplinary endeavor studies, documents, and advances solutions to help protect the planet's essential ecosystems.

For the Amazon Expedition, teams led by National Geographic Explorers spread out from the Andes to the Atlantic to explore the Amazon Basin's vast ecosystem. These scientists, community members, and storytellers studied, photographed,

▸ **2019** Climate scientists use a special drill to take a core sample of the ice at 26,000 feet on Everest's South Col.

and documented glaciers, clouds, people, waterways, vegetation, and wildlife ranging from Andean bears to river dolphins.

The Mountain Expeditions literally aimed higher, exploring alpine environments in the Hindu Kush–Himalaya and the southern Andes to understand how a changing climate affects even these seemingly remote peaks. Along the way, the expedition's members set records by installing five of the highest weather stations in the world on Mount Everest.

▲ **2022** Peru's Ausangate region is inhabited by llama- and alpaca-herding communities, which constitute some of the few remaining pastoralist societies in the world.

The third and most extensive endeavor within the multiyear project, Perpetual Planet Ocean Expeditions, targets nothing less than all five of the world's ocean basins: Arctic, Atlantic, Pacific, Southern, and Indian. Although these seas account for more than 90 percent of the world's biosphere, they are still woefully understudied. Indeed, National Geographic Explorer Katy Croff Bell found that only 0.001 percent of the deep seafloor has been visually observed. Working with other Explorers, she is devising inexpensive ways for communities to learn more about the ocean just off their shores.

▲ **2025** Teina Rongo, lead scientist for Kōrero o te 'Ōrau, an environmental group in the Cook Islands, searches for crown-of-thorns starfish to protect Rarotonga's reefs from this invasive species.

The National Geographic and Rolex Perpetual Planet Expeditions are adding to the scientific literature and sparking conservation, of course, but they are also bringing all of us indelible images of the people, animals, and landscapes of our wondrous world. As is the goal with every National Geographic enterprise, exploration, research, education, and storytelling work together to bring positive change to the world. ■

▲ **2021** Young members of Diving With a Purpose pose on a dive in Costa Rica.

That history is sometimes hidden beneath the waves. Tara Roberts, an Explorer in Residence, and Justin Dunnavant, an Explorer, are members of the maritime archaeology group Diving With a Purpose (DWP), a nonprofit organization training divers to investigate shipwrecked slave vessels around the world. Though their backgrounds differ—Roberts's is in journalism and Dunnavant's is in archaeology—they both were drawn to DWP's mission of working with local people and other divers of color to uncover lost stories of the slave trade. Their work has yielded articles, photographs, podcasts, and scientific papers. In 2022 Roberts was named Rolex National Geographic Explorer of the Year.

The following year Shabana Basij-Rasikh, a champion of education for Afghan girls, was named Rolex National Geographic Explorer of the Year. Raised during the first Taliban regime in Afghanistan, Basij-Rasikh managed to attain an education by dressing like a boy. In 2016 she founded a boarding school for girls, SOLA—School of Leadership, Afghanistan—only to have it shut down when the Taliban returned to power in 2021 and forbade women from pursuing an education past the primary grades.

▼ **2023** After the Taliban takeover in 2021, SOLA students and staff were evacuated to Kigali, Rwanda, where a new campus was established.

Basij-Rasikh did not give up. She shepherded more than 250 members of the SOLA community (including more than 100 students) to Rwanda, established the school there, and launched an online program as well, called SOLAx. Designed for Afghan girls but free to anyone, the coursework when completed gives the student a secure digital

◂ **2018** "How can SOLA reach more girls?" Shabana Basij-Rasikh has wondered. With the support of National Geographic, SOLA has launched a mobile classroom that's free to anyone, anywhere in the world.

certificate. "The secret to a peaceful and prosperous Afghanistan is no secret at all," she told National Geographic. "It's educated girls."

Explorer Victoria Herrmann is also balancing loss and renewal. As a geographer and storyteller, she works with local leaders at historic sites around the world that are threatened by the storms, floods, wildfires, and droughts of a changing environment. Her current project, Preserving Legacies, has identified endangered locations ranging from the Brazilian coast to Cambodia's Angkor Wat and trains local leaders to put environmental solutions into effect—before it's too late.

As Herrmann's project underscores, human history—and humanity's future—can't be disentangled from the natural world. Indeed, "our human story over the next several decades," says Explorer and freshwater expert Sandra Postel, director of the Global Water Policy Project, "will be to no small degree a water story." With that deep connection between water and life in mind, the Society

▾ **2023** In Jordan, Preserving Legacies collaborates with local inhabitants to combine ancient flood control practices with modern technology in order to climate-proof the 2,000-year-old Petra complex.

▲ **2018** Members of the Okavango Wilderness Project observe an elephant during the Okavango Delta biodiversity survey, the final full-length examination of all major rivers in the basin.

▼ **2023** "We have a really toxic relationship with plastic," says Explorer Agustina Besada. "A relationship that is too intense, too dependent, too addictive."

launched the multiyear National Geographic Okavango Wilderness Project (NGOWP) in 2015. The Okavango River Basin, which reaches into Angola, Namibia, and Botswana, provides water to a million people and habitat to hundreds of species of birds, plants, and mammals. Led by Explorer Steve Boyes, an interdisciplinary team including nine other Explorers is surveying and documenting the dynamics of this vast resource to ensure water security for ecosystems and communities far downstream.

But even when water is plentiful, it can be riddled with pollutants. Explorer Agustina Besada founded an enterprise called Unplastify, which works with youth, companies, and governments to prevent plastic pollution, particularly in waterways. "When we throw plastic away, there is no 'away,'" she says.

Fresh water itself can be a rare commodity, especially in a changing climate with increasing demands on resources. National Geographic's World Freshwater Initiative (WFI) aims to better understand the world's water supply with the help of an ambitious interactive site. Launched in 2023, the World Water Map reveals how water demand is outpacing water supply on every spot on our planet, from the global to the community level. The WFI also funds Explorers in freshwater science,

conservation, education, and storytelling who will use the World Water Map to inform their work.

Banding together to achieve a greater good—"the increase and diffusion of geographical knowledge"—is what drew National Geographic's founders to the Cosmos Club that foggy night in January 1888. "In union there is strength," Gardiner Greene Hubbard announced to the Society's 165 members later that month, "and through the medium of a national organization, we may hope to promote geographic research in a manner that could not be accomplished by scattered individuals, or by local societies …"

Today, the Society embraces global perspectives with a focus on impact around the world. Over the course of more than 135 years its leaders have so broadened its mission that former president Jimmy Carter once declared that National Geographic had done more "to tie the people of different nations together and to let us know and understand one another" than any other organization he knew. Though much of the planet's landmass may now be charted, its poles attained, its highest mountains climbed, that same urge to join together to better understand our world—its peoples and nations, animals and plants, its deepest seas, its vast ecosystems, and place among the twirling galaxies—is more crucial than ever. ■

▲ **2023** Although people in Jochi, Peru, know the Coata River is contaminated, they still use the water; sometimes it's their only option.

▼ **2025** At the annual Explorers Festival, new Explorers from Argentina to Zimbabwe—and many countries in between—are welcomed into the fold.

CREDITS

AUTHORS: Mark Collins Jenkins, Patricia Daniels, and Rachel Hartigan

Cover, Carsten Peter; back cover (LE to RT), Hugo van Lawick; Stephen Alvarez; Mark Fisher; Anand Varma; 2, Gordon Wiltsie; 4, Volkmar Wentzel; 6, Al Giddings; 8, National Geographic Image Collection; 10, Stanley Meltzoff; 11 (UP), Peter Bissett/Grosvenor Collection; 11 (LO), Robert S. Oakes; 12 (UP), William Henry Holmes; 12 (LO), Greely Papers, Library of Congress; 13 (UP), Mark Thiessen, NGP; 13 (LO), from *Tent Life in Siberia,* G.P. Putnam & Sons, 1910; 14, Robert E. Peary Collection; 16-7, Eliza R. Scidmore; 18 (UP), Natural History Archive/Alamy Stock Photo; 18 (LO), Mark Thiessen, NGP; 19 (UP), National Geographic Archives; 19 (LO), Harris & Ewing; 20 (UP), I.C. Russell Collection, U.S. Geological Survey; 20 (LO) and 21 (UP), Mark Thiessen, NGP; 21 (LO), Asst. Paymaster J.Q. Lovell, USN; 22 (UP), Alexander Graham Bell Collection; 22 (LO) and 23 (UP), Grosvenor Collection; 23 (LO), Robin Siegel; 24 (UP), courtesy DC Public Library, The People's Archive; 24 (LO), Eliza R. Scidmore; 25 (UP), John Alexander Douglas McCurdy; 25 (LO), National Geographic Archives; 26 (UP), U.S. National Archives; 26 (LO), Robert E. Peary Collection; 27 (UP), Mark Thiessen, NGP; 27 (LO), Rebecca Hale, NGP; 28 (UP), Donald B. MacMillan; 28 (LO), George F. Mobley; 29 (UP), Robert F. Benson; 29 (LO), National Geographic Archives; 30, Edward S. Curtis; 30-1, Charles D. Walcott; 31, George Shiras 3d; 32 (UP), Robert E. Peary Collection; 32 (LO), National Geographic Archives; 33 (UP), Lawrence Martin; 33 (LO), Mark Thiessen, NGP; 34 (UP), Rebecca Hale, NGP; 34 (LO), Otto Whitehead; 35 (UP), Christina Krysto; 35 (LO), National Geographic Archives; 36, Joseph F. Rock; 38-9, Franklin Price Knott; 40 (UP), B. Anthony Stewart; 40 (LO), Mark Thiessen, NGP; 41 (UP), George Rinhart/Corbis via Getty Images; 41 (LO), National Geographic Image Collection; 42, Franklin Price Knott; 43 (UP), Oscar D. Von Engeln; 43 (LO), Mark Thiessen, NGP; 44 (UP), Charles Martin; 44 (LO), W.H. Longley and Charles Martin; 45 (UP), Maynard Owen Williams; 45 (LO), Mark Thiessen, NGP; 46 (UP LE and LO LE), Rebecca Hale, NGP; 46 (RT), Howell Walker; 47 (UP), Maynard Owen Williams; 47 (LO), National Geographic Archives; 48 (UP), W. Robert Moore; 48 (LO), N.C. Wyeth; 49 (UP), White House collection, photo by Joseph D. Lavenburg; 49 (LO), B. Anthony Stewart; 50 (UP), © Harold Edgerton/MIT courtesy Palm Press, Inc.; 50 (LO), David Knudsen; 51 (UP), Tom Lovell; 51 (LO), H. Lee Wells, Jr.; 52 (LE), Richard H. Stewart; 52 (RT), Charles Martin; 53 (UP LE), Albert Moldvay; 53 (UP RT), James L. Stanfield; 53 (LO), Robin Siegel; 54-5, Luis Marden; 56 (UP LE), National Geographic Archives; 56 (UP RT), Thomas Nebbia; 56 (LO), National Geographic Archives; 57 (UP), Howell Walker; 57 (LO), National Geographic Archives; 58, Wilbur E. Garrett; 60-1, Hugo van Lawick; 62 (UP), Barry Bishop; 62 (LO), National Geographic Archives; 63 (UP), Robin Siegel; 63 (LO), Mark Thiessen, NGP; 64 (UP), Thomas J. Abercrombie; 64 (LO, BOTH), Mark Thiessen, NGP; 65 (UP), Thomas J. Abercrombie; 65 (LO), Robert B. Goodman; 66 (UP), Robert F. Sisson; 66 (LO), Pat McGinnis; 67, Robin Siegel; 68 (LE), Gilbert H. Grosvenor; 68 (RT), Ray V. Davis; 69 (UP), Frank Craighead; 69 (LO), John Burcham; 70 (UP), National Geographic Maps; 70 (LO), Dean Conger for NASA; 71 (UP), Edwin L. Wisherd; 71 (LO), NASA/William Taub; 72 (UP), Vincent Di Fate; 72 (LO LE), Charlie Archambault; 72 (LO RT), Bruce Dale; 73 (UP),

Wilbur E. Garrett; 73 (LO), Edwin S. Grosvenor; 74, Samuel C. Silverstein; 75 (UP), Bradford Washburn; 75 (LO, BOTH), Robin Siegel; 76 (UP), W.L. Newton III; 76 (LO), National Geographic Archives; 77 (UP), Charles Allmon; 77 (LO), W. Robert Moore; 78, Dian Fossey; 80-1, Steve Raymer; 82 (UP), Dewitt Jones; 82 (LO), Mark Thiessen, NGP; 83 (UP), James P. Blair; 83 (LO), Rebecca Hale, NGP; 84 (UP), Emory Kristof; 84 (LO), Cotton Coulson; 85 (UP), National Geographic Archives; 85 (LO), Leroy Woodson; 86 (UP), Emory Kristof; 86 (LO LE), Rebecca Hale, NGP; 86 (LO RT), George B. Schaller; 87 (UP), Albert Moldvay; 87 (LO), Luis Marden; 88 (BOTH), Mark Thiessen, NGP; 89 (UP), James L. Stanfield; 89 (LO), Steve McCurry; 90 (UP LE), Joseph D. Lavenburg; 90 (UP RT), Reinhold Messner Archives; 90 (LO), Rebecca Hale, NGP; 91 (UP), Dean Conger; 91 (LO), James L. Stanfield; 92 (UP LE), Bruce Dale; 92 (UP RT), Emory Kristof; 92 (LO), Bill Ballenberg; 93 (BOTH), O. Louis Mazzatenta; 94, David Doubilet; 95 (UP), Mark Thiessen, NGP; 95 (CTR), Robert S. Oakes; 95 (LO), Al Giddings; 96 (UP LE), Mark Thiessen, NGP; 96 (UP RT), Dr. Barry Filshie and Colin Beaton; 96 (LO), Lloyd K. Townsend and Ellen Kuzdro; 97 (UP), Jonathan Blair; 97 (LO), B. Anthony Stewart; 98 (UP), Gordon Gahan; 98 (LO), Mark Thiessen, NGP; 99 (UP LE), Sisse Brimberg; 99 (UP RT), NASA; 99 (LO), National Geographic Maps; 100, AP Photo/Keystone/Fabrice Coffrini; 102-3, Will Steger; 104 (UP LE), National Geographic Archives; 104 (UP RT), Bill Curtsinger; 104 (LO), William Albert Allard; 105 (UP), Bobby Model; 105 (LO), Gordon Wiltsie; 106, Gordon Gahan; 107 (UP), Stephen Alvarez; 107 (CTR), Ira Block; 107 (LO), Kenneth Garrett; 108 (UP), Jim Richardson; 108 (LO), Rebecca Hale, NGP; 109 (UP LE), photo by Ira Block, model by Brian Cooley; 109 (UP RT), American Museum of Natural History; 109 (LO), Annie Griffiths; 110 (LE, BOTH), National Geographic Archives; 110 (RT), Carsten Peter; 111 (UP), Frans Lanting; 111 (LO), National Geographic Archives; 112 (UP), David Doubilet; 112 (LO), National Geographic Books; 113 (UP), National Geographic; 113 (LO), George Steinmetz; 114 (UP), William Thompson; 114 (LO), James Nifong; 115 (UP), Bill Hatcher; 115 (LO), National Geographic Archives; 116, Ronan Donovan; 117 (UP), David Doubilet; 117 (LO LE), George Grall; 117 (LO RT), Bianca Lavies; 118 (UP), Michael Nichols; 118 (LO LE), Mark Thiessen, NGP; 118 (LO RT), Michael Nichols; 119, Sam Abell; 120 (LE), Mark Thiessen, NGP; 120 (RT), Krithi Karanth; 121 (UP), Avi Kalpfer; 121 (LO), Brian Skerry; 122, Tommy Heinrich; 123 (UP), Mark Thiessen, NGP; 123 (LO), Meoita/Shutterstock; 124 (UP LE), Beverly Joubert; 124 (UP RT), NASA, ESA, and the Hubble SM4 ERO Team; 124 (LO), National Geographic Archives; 125 (UP), Kent Kobersteen; 125 (LO), National Geographic Books; 126, Jason Gulley; 128-9, Robbie Shone; 130 (UP), Jimmy Chin; 130 (LO), Mikey Schaefer; 131 (UP), National Geographic Society, 2026; 131 (LO), National Geographic Society, 2025; 132 (UP), Luján Agusti; 132 (CTR), Marcio Pimenta; 132 (LO), model by Santiago Reuil; 133 (UP), Brent Stirton/Getty Images; 133 (LO), Rebecca Hale, NGP; 134 (UP), Sharon Guynup; 134 (LO), Steve Winter; 135 (UP), Alisha Vasudev; 135 (LO LE), Jaime Rojo; 135 (LO RT), Spencer Lowell; 136 (BOTH), Luján Agusti; 137 (UP), Brian Skerry; 137 (LO), Rebecca Hale, NGP; 138 (UP), Babak Tafreshi; 138 (LO) and 139 (UP), John Stanmeyer; 139 (LO), Madelyn Arnold; 140, Dirk Collins; 141 (UP), Thomas P. Peschak; 141 (LO), Giacomo d'Orlando; 142 (UP), Wayne Lawrence; 142 (LO), Yagazie Emezi; 143 (UP), courtesy SOLA; 143 (LO), Michael O. Snyder; 144 (UP), Anand Varma; 144 (LO), Rebecca Hale, NGP; 145 (UP), Musuk Nolte; 145 (LO), Rebecca Hale, NGP.

INDEX

Boldface indicates illustrations.

Since 1888, the National Geographic Society has funded more than 15,000 research, conservation, education, technology, and storytelling projects around the world. National Geographic Partners distributes a portion of the funds it receives from your purchase to National Geographic Society to support their mission to illuminate and protect the wonder of our world.

National Geographic Partners, LLC
1145 17th Street NW
Washington, DC 20036-4688 USA

Get closer to National Geographic Explorers and photographers, and connect with our global community. Join us today at nationalgeographic.org/joinus

For rights or permissions inquiries, please contact National Geographic Books Subsidiary Rights: bookrights@natgeo.com

ISBN: 978-1-4262-2482-9

This book is financially supported by the National Geographic Society.

Portions of this book were previously published in *On Assignment With National Geographic.*

The authorized representative in the EU for product safety and compliance is Disney Trading B.V., Asterweg 15S, 1031 HL, Amsterdam, The Netherlands
email: DCP.DL-EU.bookscontact@disney.com

Printed in the United States of America
26/VP/1

ABOUT THE NATIONAL GEOGRAPHIC SOCIETY

The National Geographic Society is a global nonprofit organization that uses the power of science, exploration, education, and storytelling to illuminate and protect the wonder of our world.

Since 1888, the Society has pushed the boundaries of exploration to better understand our world. We have awarded more than 15,000 grants to National Geographic Explorers—scientists, conservationists, innovators, educators, and storytellers—for work across all seven continents. Today, Explorers are advancing new knowledge and leading conservation programs with outsize impact to protect nature, wildlife, historical places, and communities. They're documenting the wonder of our world—including its beauty, mystery, and the threats it faces—and inspiring people to care and act on behalf of our planet and its people.

The Society supports remarkable individuals whose groundbreaking work is shaping the future of exploration, education, conservation, and storytelling, celebrating excellence, and fostering innovation within the global network of Explorers and beyond. The more opportunities people have to understand the natural and cultural worlds, the more inspired they are to protect it.

Covering more than 135 years of history, *In the Field With National Geographic* has only scratched the surface of the everlasting impact of our work inspiring people to preserve and protect the world around them. To learn even more about our work and how you can join us, visit us at our Museum of Exploration in Washington, D.C., or online at natgeo.com/impact.